THE
BUSINESS-EXIT
ROLLER COASTER

THE
BUSINESS-EXIT
ROLLER COASTER

Confidential Conversations with Business
Owners About the Most Important
Financial Decision of Their Lives

BRANDON JACOB, CPA
M&A Advisor
MATT MICHEL
Serial Entrepreneur

Copyright © 2026 by Brandon Jacob and Matt Michel.

All rights reserved. Designed and printed in the United States of America. No part of this book may be used or reproduced in any manner whatsoever without written permission except in the case of brief quotations embodied in critical articles and reviews. For information, contact:

Coldstream Press
601 Paradise Cove
Denton, TX 76208

ISBN: 979-8-218-91069-3

The information provided in this book is for informational purposes only and is not intended to be a source of legal advice or financial advice with respect to the material presented. The information and/or documents contained in this book do not constitute legal or financial advice and should never be used without first consulting with a lawyer or financial professional to determine what may be best for your individual needs.

The publisher and the author do not make any guarantee or other promise as to any results that may be obtained from using the content of this book. You should never make any investment decision without first consulting with your own financial advisor and conducting your own research and due diligence. To the maximum extent permitted by law, the publisher and the author disclaim any and all liability in the event any information, commentary, analysis, opinions, advice and/or recommendations contained in this book prove to be inaccurate, incomplete or unreliable, or result in any investment or other losses.

Content contained or made available through this book is not intended to and does not constitute legal advice or and no attorney-client relationship is formed. The publisher and the author are providing this book and its contents on an "as is" basis. Your use of the information in this book is at your own risk.

Designed and printed in the USA

Contents

From the Authors: Why This Book Is Needed		1
Introduction		9
What Was Learned		17
I	**Motives**	**27**
1	Investor Return	30
2	Investment	32
3	Family/Partner Buyouts	34
4	Family Pressure	36
5	Marital Strife	37
6	Health	38
7	Death	40
8	Burnout	42
9	Risk Avoidance	45
10	Changing Business Environment	48
11	Fear	51
12	Retirement	53
13	Money	55
14	Insufficient Motives	57
II	**Getting to the LOI**	**61**
15	Uncertainty	65
16	Seller's Representative	67
17	M&A Team	70
18	Betrayals	73
19	Management Meetings	75
20	Intimidation	78
21	Valuation	81
22	Multiples	86
23	Earn-Outs	88
24	Hold-Backs	91
25	Seller Notes	93
26	Restrictive Agreements	96
27	Building Access	99

28	Negotiatins	101
29	Equity Rolls	104
30	Selecting a Buyer	108
31	Reading in Team Members	113
32	Team Concerns	119

III	**Getting to Close**	**123**
33	Due Diligence	125
34	Deal Falls Through	130
35	Quality of Earnings Report	133
36	Maintaining Performance	136
37	Stay-On Bonuses	138
38	Key Employee Departure	139
39	Coping Methods	141
40	Second Thoughts	142
41	The Close	144
42	Funding	147
43	Relief	150
44	Owner Rewards	152
45	Team Rewards	154
46	Taxes	157

IV	**Winding Down**	**161**
47	Staying On	163
48	Focusing on Strengths	166
49	Learning Opportunities	169
50	Corporate Suits	171
51	Reports and Meetings	174
52	Buyer Decisions	176
53	Time to Leave	180
54	Walking Away	184
55	Retirement Parties	186
56	Loss of Identity	187
57	New Purpose	190
58	Depression	194
59	Remorse	196
60	Post-Sale Conflict	200
61	Staying Busy	202

62	Income Streams	204
63	Former Employees	206
64	Travel	208
65	Buyer Mistakes	210
66	Wealth	212
67	Estate Planning	218
68	Relationships	221

Appendices 223

Miscellaneous Business Tips for Owners Who Want to Sell	224
50 Truths About Selling a Business	227
Industries Represented Among the Respondents	233

About the Authors 235

A Message from Matt Michel

What No One Tells You About the Emotions of Selling Your Business

What you **MUST KNOW** *before making the most important financial decision of your life*

"Hang on," came the voice of our investment banker over my truck's Bluetooth speaker. "He's on the other line and calling me from Europe. I'll call you back."

He hung up and I turned to the COO in the passenger seat. He shrugged. "They'll hit the number or they won't. We've already got the offer we need."

We were driving in circles because the office wasn't soundproof enough. We'd done that a lot over the past few months as we proceeded with the plan to sell the business I started 15 years earlier. I was worn out by the process, by the emotional highs, lows, frustrations, aggravations, and even the happy surprises. But we were close to a deal with the company we thought offered the best fit, so despite a weariness that reminded me of being a player near the end of a long sports season, there was incredible excitement. It felt like the moments before the start of the championship game.

The investment banker called back and explained their counteroffer. It wasn't quite as good as the best offer we had, but it was better than our shareholders expected, and this buyer represented a better fit for our team.

I looked at the COO. We both nodded. "Tell him we've got a deal," I said. The COO and I high-fived. We had won the championship.

I knew we still faced due diligence, but we already did a quality of earnings report, so I wondered how much worse due diligence could be. In my naivete, I thought the worst part was over. Instead, the *best* part was over. For me, this was the highlight. We had a buyer and agreed on a price. It couldn't get much better. It was all the highs and possibilities, but none of the lows. In truth, the game had barely begun. It would get a lot more painful and frustrating, so much so that I nearly walked off the field more than once. I had done it before during failed attempts to sell the company, but never after getting past the letter of intent, or LOI.

When this buyer sent me their LOI it was the fifth time I'd been presented with one. It was the first one I'd signed. By this time, I knew a lot about the mechanics of selling a company, but I wasn't prepared for the emotional side, and it hit me hard. Many of the people we interviewed for this book described it as an *emotional roller coaster*. It is. It starts with the recognition that it's time to sell and it doesn't end until you walk away and find something else to do with your life.

After I left my business—which was no longer mine—I talked about the emotional swings with Brandon Jacob, a good friend, CPA, and independent mergers & acquisitions (M&A) consultant. He guides a lot of business owners through the sale of their companies and said he wished there were a book he could hand people so they would know what to expect as they begin the process of selling their businesses. *There must be a book like that,* I thought.

But when I looked for such a book, I couldn't find one. Brandon suggested we write it. We followed an empirical research methodology and conducted confidential, in-depth interviews with nearly a hundred business owners, buyers, and sellers' representatives. Every owner and transaction is different, but common themes emerged during the interviews. This book is organized around those themes. It's not a wordy book. When I was a marketing consultant, I used to joke that I weighed the final reports on a scale for content. By contrast, this book is written to be easily read by busy business owners to prepare them for the roller coaster of emotions that accompany the sale of a business and the life afterwards.

Selling a business isn't like selling a car. It's more like selling your firstborn child. If you don't manage the emotional aspects correctly, they can be disastrous. They can blow up a deal. They can also blow up a life. While most sellers reported a sense of relief at funding, depression in the months after was far from uncommon. I know I went through it.

Jacob and Michel

As someone who has guided others through the sales process, and someone who experienced it, Brandon and I believe this book fills an unmet need. It's an essential book for anyone contemplating the sale of a business.

Matt Michel
Speaker/Writer/Rancher
214.995.8889

A Message from Brandon Jacob

Why This Book Is Needed

The CEO of a large, publicly traded company agreed to allocate an hour or so to meet my client, a very nervous owner of a small, privately held, second-generation business that he was ready to sell and retire. The owner, 63 at the time, didn't have children and his key employees were past the age where a sale to them made sense, so a third-party sale was his best option.

My client reminded me almost daily that he wanted all of his employees to have jobs with the new owner. He also lost no opportunity to make this demand clear when interacting with the buyer's representatives. Despite all of the conversations we'd had, in which I stressed that the highly sought-after and valued technicians he employed were a key element in the buyer's purchasing decision, my client made "taking care of his employees" his daily battle cry.

Soon, we were under a letter of intent. Because of the size of the transaction, due diligence was not going to be horrific. All my client had to do was control his emotions and make it through a meeting with the prospective CEO.

We arrived early and went over our notes. I reminded him that the buyer understood his concerns for his employees. I said, "Please don't make this a topic today. The buyer heard you loud and clear, multiple times, and he's getting tired addressing it over and over. They got it." He agreed and we settled in for the meeting.

The other team took their seats. I broke the ice with the customary friendly chit-chat. Unfortunately, my client's mind was set and, even though he was paying me for my professional counsel, he hadn't listened. As soon as the chatter ended my client demanded, "First thing I want to make sure of is that my employees are taken care of."

This was the moment I had the idea for this book. I had worked hard to get my client to the point of a sale, but he wouldn't take my advice. By letting his emotions lead him, he was jeopardizing a truly good opportunity for his employees and himself.

The Business-Exit Roller Coaster

The sale of a business, especially a second- or third-generation business, is a significant emotional moment. The decision to sell, the process of selling and then, ultimately, the actual sale, bring out every emotion: stress, anxiety, betrayal, guilt, joy, relief, happiness, regret, suspicion. Representing business owners as they navigate through the process involves managing all of these and more. Seller's representatives add value when they anticipate and address areas where business owners will get bogged down.

After the meeting, and some reassurance to the buyer that my client was stable, the transaction proceeded and ultimately closed. The employees were welcomed and hired by the buyers, the customers continued to receive the service they had come to expect, and my client retired after a one-year transition (which included the achievement of an earn-out). The transaction was successful, but harder than it should have been. In fact, the night before the close, I had to convince the seller that the buyer really *was* interested in buying his business. The following evening, after the close, I had to tell my client that the buyer really does need access to his building and employees, something he was trying to delay.

While this business owner was a little over-the-top, others have been similarly stymied during the sales process. *Will the buyer want my employees? How will confidentiality work? What will they expect of me? Really, how hard is due diligence?*

These are just some of the concerns I've encountered over the years. There are millions of how-to books about selling a business, but few acknowledge the hard questions that all business owners come up with. If a business owner could pull information from those who went before—not from one friend who sold and is now the "expert," but a panel of owners who sold—the owner would be better prepared for the sales process and the emotional ups and downs. *The Business-Exit Roller Coaster* is just that: a summary of the tales of nearly 100 former business owners in many different industries, all of whom have been through the process, as well as the experiences of buyers and seller's representatives.

This book ...

1. Reassures owners of privately held businesses that they could sell their companies, regardless of industry, size, or geographic location. This book is more than just a business rah-rah. The affirmation that anyone can successfully sell a

business provides valuable insight that will be needed when the dealing gets rough.

2. Addresses common emotional swings that all sellers have. For every business owner, the sale of a business has emotional highs and lows. Not all sellers share the same emotions. This book attempts to address them all.

3. Helps make it happen. So many would-be former owners continue to own and operate their businesses simply because they are unable to make hard, up-front decisions. This book addresses the *Why do I want to sell?* types of questions, the emotional pitfalls, and the landmines that keep owners from moving into each phase of the process.

4. Makes it enjoyable. You may only sell one business in your lifetime. It can either be a great experience or a horrific one. Imagine going through it with an understanding of the end result and how to handle the unknowns. This book provides the insight so that the first business sale—for many, the *only* business sale—seems like the second one.

5. Addresses the aftermath, the potential negatives of selling a business, and the challenges that come from walking away and starting a new chapter in a business owner's life.

If you're selling a business, or helping someone else sell one, you've come to the right place.

Brandon Jacob, CPA
Contractors Financial Opportunity, LLC
ContractorsCFO.com
713.443.8311

Introduction

People sell businesses every day. If this is their first time, the seller will be faced with many emotions, positive and negative, and many questions that, up until reading this book, might seem like issues that no one else has faced. The truth is that everyone who takes the journey of selling a business faces the same questions and the same emotions. "The entire acquisition process," noted one buyer, "is just wrought with crazy emotions, high and low on so many levels." And when emotions become extreme and the business owner is caught unprepared, mistakes are made, mistakes that affect a marriage, future generations, or the seller's own contentment after the sale is complete and it's time to move on with life.

Inexperience equates to unknowns. Unknowns lead to fear. If a would-be seller can learn from the experience of other sellers before engaging in the business-sales process, the seller will enjoy the process more and be more successful at it.

Strap In for an Emotional Roller Coaster Ride!

Selling a business, especially a multi-generational one, can involve a LOT of raw emotions and soul-searching. As one private-equity investor explained, "Normally, I'm dealing with how Grandpa would feel about this if he was alive. I'm dealing with how Aunt Sue and how Aunt Judy are going to take it and feel about it. I'm dealing with them wondering if they're doing the right thing for their kids and future generations. Ninety percent of what I do is dealing with emotions and helping people get right with it."

Overall, the process of selling a business was often described as a roller coaster ride. One business owner's comments were typical: "Yeah. It's like a roller coaster. You go through all these machinations and then get to the big hill. You're right at the top. You think, we're doing it! This is done. It's going to happen, and we're going to enjoy the ride."

The Business-Exit Roller Coaster

Another business owner talked about *multiple* roller coaster rides. He said, "Our family rode through the roller coaster for quite a while. We wanted to kind of make sure that this wasn't just a temporary emotion. One or two of us wanted to do it. We all decided that this was an all-or-nothing thing. Once we got to the point where we all agreed that, yes, we want to go forward with it, it was just a different roller coaster that we were getting on. Once we actually started getting some basic offers, and then we went under LOI with the first organization, it was, 'Holy cow, like, this could actually happen!' It was a very, very different roller coaster."

One thing's for sure: Sellers will blossom throughout the process and become mini experts by the time the sale is consummated and the wire transfer is made. The rookie business seller becomes a veteran and the initial fears and concerns are cast aside. It's one more reward at the end of the journey.

How to Read This Book

The Business-Exit Roller Coaster is written in the order most business sales take place, but every sale is different. If a chapter isn't relevant to you, skip it. If a chapter addresses an issue you're facing right now, jump to it. It's all spelled out in the table of contents. Do what makes sense for you.

The ideal time to read this book is before going to market or in the early stages of a sale. For most, selling a business is a very emotional decision, one with significant financial implications. It's when the emotions swing to extremes that the financial outcomes may not be maximized and unforced errors might occur. Because this book is based on conversations with many business owners, buyers, and sellers' representatives, contradictory experiences and emotions were noted. When conflicting experiences were encountered, they were all presented to paint a realistic portrait of the range of emotions and outcomes.

While a diverse group of businesses are represented, the themes and emotions are remarkably consistent. It mattered little where a business was physically located, whether it operated locally or internationally, or whether it employed a few or a few hundred people. It didn't matter if it was a family operation, a partnership, or had more of a corporate structure; whether it was in home services, professional practices, software, agriculture, or manufacturing. The emotions are almost universally consistent.

The chapters are summarized in a section entitled "What We Learned." The original intent was to put this section at the end of the book as a wrap-up, but we realized it would be more helpful at the beginning. Read this section first for initial clarity and then proceed to the chapters.

Next, let's look at the types of buyers a seller is likely to encounter along the way.

Types of Buyers

Nearly 100 former business owners were interviewed for this book. The following types of buyers were found to be the most common.

- Private Individuals
- Family
- Employees
- Private Equity
- Strategic Buyers
- Search Equity
- Serial Entrepreneurs
- Competitors

Private Individuals

Typically, the private individual is someone who previously sold a business and is now looking for a new venture. Private individuals may or may not have a geographic or industry focus and may not understand the mechanics involved in completing a transaction. Worse, a private individual may come to you with inadequate capital. Sellers shouldn't be tempted to give a discount and should be quick to disengage at the first sign of an inability to complete the transaction. Private individuals should be pre-qualified, and sellers should get an understanding of their funding capabilities.

Family

Selling a family business to family members makes sense and it happens every day. This is how businesses become multi-generational, when a father and mother sell their business to a child or other relative. The emotional roller coaster when selling to a family member typically involves fewer ups and downs, but the ones that remain are no less challenging. Perhaps the greatest challenge is making the critical determination that the would-be family member has both the desire and the capability to own and operate the business.

In other cases, a family member checks the desire and the capability boxes but lacks the necessary capital. If the business is small and profitable enough, the seller might offer to finance the sale with a note. Luckily, there are also options available through banks that provide loans supported by the Small Business Administration (SBA). An SBA-supported loan can be a useful form of capital when selling to a family member or employee.

When a family business becomes too large or too valuable to justify a sale to a relative, a third-party buyer is usually brought in. Also, businesses operating in highly desirable industries may find that a sale to a third party could yield significantly more than the fair market value. Even if a family member is willing to step up and pay more than this, there is a point where the elevated purchase price cannot be justified.

Employees

Many small business owners "reward" a loyal employee with the opportunity to take ownership. The challenge is that many employees aren't capable of owning and operating a business and they don't fully consider the risks, sacrifices, and uncertainties that come along with the privilege and responsibilities of being called the owner. Care must be taken in the way an employee is approached and how discussions are held. If the dream of ownership takes root and then goes away, the drive to be a good employee often goes with it.

The probability of an employee following through with the opportunity to buy the business declines with age and personal responsibilities. It's unlikely that the 50+ year old general manager with one or more children in college will have the risk appetite to purchase a business. If he does, and lacks the cash for a down payment, he'll probably be reluctant to take out a home equity loan to fund the purchase.

A good employee buyer is a young, hungry employee with high aspirations and entrepreneurial drive. While this buyer will see the deal through, he'll often lack the necessary capital. The seller should be ready to finance all or part of the sale as well as explore options for the employee with the SBA.

Private Equity

Think of private equity (PE) as individual groups of investors who have raised private funds with the intention of buying, improving, growing, and then selling businesses. PE has the funds readily available to complete a negotiated transaction.

While private equity can get a negative rap, they are excellent buyers and may be willing to pay a higher purchase price. PE buyers are sophisticated. Business owners aren't going to slip anything past them. Due diligence will feel more intensive than a full IRS audit. Sellers shouldn't deal with private equity without being represented by an intermediary, such as a broker, a mergers & acquisitions advisor, or an investment banker.

Business owners who sell to private equity and stay on should prepare themselves for a grind. Status quo is not celebrated. Typically, PE investors hold their investments for three to ten years. From day one, the intention is to sell the business. What happens between the day of close and the day private equity sells is a never-ending quest for improvements—processes, people, revenue, and profit. Business owners who stay on should be prepared to work twice as hard as they ever have before.

Strategic Buyer

Strategic buyers present the most lucrative opportunity for business owners. For example, a parts manufacturer may be approached by a customer who wants to vertically integrate for more control over his supply chain, or a full-service software company may want to purchase a business that has developed an innovative program. A third example is a distributor who wants to expand in another state and seeks to buy an established distributor rather than start from scratch. In each of these cases, the seller fulfills a strategic need of the buyer. If the buyer has deep pockets, price becomes secondary to the need.

Strategic buyers, like private equity, are financially capable of paying an owner the full worth of a business. Otherwise, they wouldn't be looking for acquisitions in the first place. Strategic buyers may be slightly less apt to make broad-stroke changes to a business and may even take a hands-off approach, so they can be the right choice for business owners who plan to stay on.

Serial Entrepreneurs

A variant of a private investor, a serial entrepreneur is an individual who buys, builds, and sells businesses. They should be able to finance the transaction with their personal fortunes, secured lending, or a combination of both. Don't underestimate the serial entrepreneur as a buyer, nor overlook the fact that these individuals got where they are by understanding how to negotiate the terms of a transaction to fit their needs.

Search Equity

Individual buyers seeking to purchase a single business with pledges of financial support from private money are referred to as search equity. They secure pledges of financial backing to finance all or part of a business opportunity. At the onset of the search, the individual raises capital to finance living and search expenses, with pledges of funds once the right investment is found. Search equity will look at a lot of businesses and try to pay as little as possible. Typically, search funds are not industry-specific, and the fund will cast a wide net across multiple industries and will look at many possibilities simultaneously.

If a seller isn't careful, a lot of time will be spent only to find that the offer is less than expected. In addition, once a business is identified and the deal is loosely structured, it must also be agreed upon by the investors who pledged the capital. The process for approval will add time to the transaction. Then, one or more of the investors may disapprove of the business or terms. When entertaining a search fund, sellers should be sure to understand where the capital will come from before accepting a letter of intent.

Competitor

Many business owners believe the right buyer is a competitor. On the surface, this makes sense. Who better than a competitor to acquire a business and fold it into his? However, unless the acquisition propels the competitor's business significantly ahead in the market, the incentive to pay fair market value is limited. A competitor will not value all of the tangible and intangible assets because the competitor has its own. A competitor will more than likely value the customers and, to an extent, the employees. Putting all faith in selling to a competitor can be a gateway to failure.

What Was Learned
A Short Summary of the Findings

Selling a business is fraught with emotion. Owners who approach the process with eyes wide open and prepared for the ups and downs of an emotional roller coaster will experience less stress and ultimately emerge mentally healthier. The research that is the foundation of this book is not focused on techniques to get the most money, but on how to get the most satisfaction from the most important financial transaction of a lifetime.

It's the Big Game and the Stakes Have Never Been Higher

No matter how sharp a first-time business owner is, he's playing from behind and working at a disadvantage compared to seasoned buyers who have far deeper experience. Think of a golf game where an amateur and a pro are equally matched at the range. Their long, middle, and short games are almost identical. But when they take to the links, the amateur has never played the course, he's never played *any* course, and he's never played for money. The pro has played under pressure and has logged round after round on the very course they're playing. Every shot into the woods, every bad lie is a new experience for the amateur. The pressure builds and, if he lets his emotions get ahead of him, his game will suffer accordingly.

The amateur, confident in his own ability and reluctant to tip a caddy, may elect to carry his own clubs. He selects his own drivers and irons for each shot, never knowing when he makes a mistake. But if he's smart, the amateur will invest in the best caddy he can find, someone familiar with the course and who can guide him through the process of club and shot selection as well as help keep his emotions in check so that he makes fewer unforced errors. This is the role of a broker, a mergers & acquisitions advisor, or an investment bank.

When it comes to selling a business, another sports analogy applies. Think of a football game. There's the pre-game, two halves, and the post-game. The pre-game covers everything leading up to the game. Players who know they'll be starters mentally prepare themselves for the competition. They go over the game plan in their minds. They think through how they're going to respond to certain formations. Players who are low on the depth chart and don't anticipate seeing the field are less likely to prepare mentally. If they unexpectedly get called off the bench, it's confusing. They aren't ready. They're forced to play on instinct and react the best they can.

It's similar for business sellers. Those who are proactive, who made conscious decisions to sell before external factors forced a sale, were the healthiest and happiest. They were able to prepare mentally, to practice their approach, and to think through how they would react in different situations.

Unfortunately, life doesn't always wait for people to be ready. Just like injuries might thrust a third- or fourth-string player into a game, the unpredictable can happen in business. A spouse or partner can pass away. Health can fail. A business might need to be sold to save a marriage. All of these, and more, were encountered during the interviews for this book. Life can be unpredictable and unforeseen. What *is* predictable is the need to eventually exit the business. It will happen.

Everyone Exits. Choose the Exit.

Some business owners walk out vertically on their own. Some are pushed. Others are carried horizontally. No matter how they leave, everyone exits. Even if a business owner has no plans to sell his company, he should begin formulating how he'd approach the process should the unexpected happen and he's forced or pressured to sell before he's ready. He should also prepare a succession plan for his family in case he takes the ultimate premature exit.

Once the decision to sell is made the first half of the business-sales game begins. It's the process to find a buyer and ink a letter of intent, or LOI. The LOI stipulates the price, terms, and conditions of the sale. This is what most people think selling a business is all about. While it's a critical phase, it only takes you to halftime. There's much more to come.

When business owners take a DIY approach, the first half is where they're likely to make the most serious errors and omissions. Sometimes it's because they don't know what they don't know (and, even post-sale, they may not be aware of their mistakes and what they left on the table). Other times, it's because they let their emotions control their actions. It's easy to get starry-eyed about the sale price… to be overcome with fear… to be frustrated beyond belief.

Again, business owners should have an agent who works on their behalf. The agent should have "transaction experience," which means he knows what to expect. He knows how to structure a favorable transaction based on the seller's desires. He also knows what to expect emotionally. A seller's agent, whether a business broker, mergers & acquisitions advisor, or investment banker is more than a negotiator. He's also a counselor. He prepares the business owner for the twists and turns. He tamps down out-of-control emotions. He acts as a mediator between buyer and seller.

At the outset, most business owners have only a vague sense of what a business might be worth and who might be a ready buyer. Formal business valuations are theoretical. They can easily be nudged up or down. They are often out-of-date, based on historical measures, and can change dramatically from year to year.

Business values can fluctuate by industry, the number of companies for sale, the changing structure of the industry, the regulatory environment, and the presence of private equity, to name just a few factors. Many business owners get obsessed with the "multiples" of earnings. They hear about incredible numbers from peers and at industry shows, but these can be erroneous.

Business owners who take a more practical approach, deciding what they need financially to meet their personal goals and requirements, and who cheerfully accept more if they can get it, but not less, seem to emerge healthier.

This is important. Some owners get caught up in the glamour of receiving a certain multiple when the net after taxes is not enough for them to become financially secure. These owners would've been better off if they had waited and grown their companies until the proceeds of a sale could support them. Instead, they unhappily discover they need to continue to work, only now, whether they stay on with the buyer or seek employment elsewhere, they're working for someone else.

A lot of business acquisition activity over the past few years has been driven by private equity. Now, private equity may have detractors, but business owners should be raving fans. In industries with significant private equity play, owners benefit. Private equity bids up the market price. Their funds may even be willing to pay above market pricing due to their internal pressure to close deals. After all, it's hard to get a deal done.

Yet private equity can be intimidating to business owners. Investors come in speaking a different vocabulary of second bites of the apple, runways, and bio-breaks. Owners need to recognize that private equity may be populated by Ivy League financial whizzes, but most of them lack the operational chops to run the businesses they're acquiring.

Business May Be a Team Sport, but There's No Team Without the Owner

Along the way to the LOI, some business owners seem to be swept away by a tide of guilt about the impact that selling their companies will have on their employees. The owners recognize the role their teams play in helping them achieve success, but they undervalue the role they play as owners. They're the ones who accept the risk that accompanies business ownership. If a business fails, the employee loses a job while the owner loses everything. Without the business owner, there would be no jobs in the first place. Owners shouldn't feel guilty for grabbing the brass ring. They've earned it.

Owner guilt accompanies a paternalistic view that many owners take about their teams. They worry that their employees will discover they are selling. They worry that the buyer won't take care of the employees. And they dread the day of reckoning when the team must be informed. In most cases, it seems obvious that buyers are not purchasing companies to strip them of their employees, but some business owners have a tough time accepting and internalizing the obvious. Even if the buyer furloughs every employee, the employees will be fine. It's worth repeating: *The employees will be fine.*

It can be difficult to accept, but the allegiance of most employees is directly tied to their paychecks. When paychecks move to new owners, so does employee allegiance. As long as they have jobs with pay and benefits, employees tend to be indifferent about the sale of a business.

Business owners who, long before they take action, are upfront with their people seem to have an easier time. Hiding things is stressful, and outright deception raises the stress to the stratosphere. It should be no surprise that the business owners who read in their key people sooner seem to cope better.

Rumor Control and Sabotage

Secrets are hard to keep. Owners shouldn't be surprised when information about the sale leaks, and those who have communication plans in place are prepared. Positive action reduces stress.

Selling a business affects a lot of people, in and out of the company. Don't be surprised if one or more affected parties take self-interested actions that might adversely impact the owner, such as attempts to sabotage the sale, revealing information to competitors, or hurting supplier relations. These will seem like betrayals, but it's important for the business owner to let them go emotionally and keep his eyes on the prize. That's what matters.

The Big Game: First Half

When it comes time to pick a buyer, the vast majority of owners seem to want those who represent good cultural fits and who will take care of the team, customers, and suppliers exactly as the owner did. These unicorns do not exist, except possibly in sales to family members who worked in the business. In the end, culture counts, but money rules. Culture only comes into play if the money is sufficient.

On the subject of money, in most cases, up-front money is only part of the negotiation. There may be equity rolls, earn-outs, and notes. There are restraining agreements and hold-backs. The details of the deal can be confusing to business owners who are inexperienced in the process.

If they lack representation, owners selling their companies will get their information from the buyer without filters or guidance. Caught up in the emotion of the moment, with dollar signs in their eyes, they're liable to roll more equity forward than they should or to count earn-outs as part of the number they need from the sale. In short, they're prone to unforced errors. They're also prone to falling victim to bad-faith negotiators, who are rare but nevertheless exist.

When the negotiations are complete, the LOI is signed. This locks in the terms, unless there are surprises revealed in due diligence. For the business owner, this is the top of the roller coaster hill. The sale now seems real, the wealth seems within reach. It's a world of possibilities without the awareness of the pain of due diligence. But this is only halftime. The second half awaits, and fatigue will set in before the final whistle.

The Big Game: Second Half

After the LOI is signed, the real work begins. This is due diligence, the second half of the game. Business owners often struggle to meet the informational requirements of buyers, but it's when inexperienced buyers do a poor job of due diligence that post-sale conflict most often happens. In this regard, due diligence should be welcomed. It protects both the buyer and seller.

The business owner can ease the burden of due diligence by bringing in other team members to help with the information demands. Otherwise, the owner will place himself under needless stress and will sleepwalk for months due to simple weariness.

Make no mistake: Due diligence is a grind. It can seem overwhelming and unrelenting. The demands lead some owners to take their eyes off immediate business performance, creating even more stress. While due diligence is occurring, owners must figure out a way to double down on company metrics, keeping sales up and profit strong. Despite the grind, due diligence is no time to ease up on business performance. Owners will have time to relax after the sale.

As if that weren't enough, a key employee will often choose the worst possible time to have a meltdown and leave the company. Employees leave all the time. Buyers understand and accept this, yet business owners tend to magnify the talent deficit that a missing employee creates, placing even more stress on the owner. Instead, they should accept the possibility that key people might leave. They should remain confident in their ability to find a replacement. Some owners mitigate the potential for defections with stay-on bonuses, payable at or after close. No one is irreplaceable, not even the owner.

Some owners fret and stress throughout due diligence. They worry that something will cause the deal to blow up. Something might. Sales do fall apart. It's healthy for owners to mentally prepare for the possibility so it doesn't destroy them if it happens. Owners should always remember that there are other buyers. If one doesn't work out another one will.

Jacob and Michel

The Big Game: The Clock Runs Out

Due diligence eventually ends. After all of the build-up, the close of the transaction is completely anticlimactic. For most, it's a five-minute phone call or video conference. Funding, which follows the close, is anything but anticlimactic. When the wire transfer occurs and the business owner sees the money in his account, he realizes his life has changed forever. He's done it. He shows his spouse and they're both stunned by the number, even if expected. It's no longer an abstraction. Seeing it makes it real.

Many business owners, maybe the majority, feel incredible relief with the close. The stress is over. Due diligence is over. The grind is done. The debt and personal guarantees of the owner are satisfied. The risk of tort litigation and employee lawsuits ends. The fear that everything will fall apart before the business can be sold evaporates. The pressure of payroll is over. The complaints of employees and customers are directed to someone else. The owner who sells a business has done what few accomplish: He has successfully operated and sold a business. He has completed the entrepreneurial odyssey, the full arc of business ownership.

Post-Game

The close and funding doesn't signal the end of the transaction. The post-game remains. In fact, for many business owners, the greatest emotional challenges are still on the horizon.

The reality of turning over the reins of a business can be difficult. For most owners, the business is more than a company. It's a part of themselves. It's like giving away a daughter in marriage. It's like part of their body is amputated. They feel pain from a missing body part that's no longer there. Owners must expect the buyer to do things differently and to do things the owner doesn't agree with. The buyer may even wreck the company. It's the buyer's company now, not the former owner's. Fortunately, the owner can take consolation from his fat bank account and newly enriched investment portfolio.

Second thoughts are common. Sellers often experience some remorse, but rarely enough that they would willingly take the company back and return the proceeds. Apparently, remorse has its limits.

Some give financial rewards to everyone on their teams. Others limit the rewards to key people. Some don't receive enough to spread the money around. Business owners who could afford to share some of the proceeds seemed to feel good about taking care of their people. They may have complained a little about the cost, but they felt it was a small price in the long run.

Some owners stay on after the sale, but these stays tend to be limited. It's hard for owners to accept subordinate positions, especially in companies they built. It's hard to support and promote decisions they might disagree with. It's hard to become an employee. Many remove themselves. In other cases, the buyer makes it obvious it's time for the old owner to go. It seems that too much self-employment does make a person unemployable.

The happiest owners who stay on after the sale are those who mentally give up any pretense of control and look at this time as a learning opportunity. While an owner may know his business, he looks forward to learning about the buyers' business. The owner can succeed if he learns how to bite his tongue and deal with buyers who know less about his business than he does, but who think otherwise. They also have to adjust to the meetings and reports that accompany a larger enterprise. If they can't manage this, if they struggle, they should leave. It's not healthy to stay.

Leaving It All on the Field

When it's time to walk away, there appears to be a divergence between introverts and extroverts. The former have an easier time separating themselves and their identities from the business. They are less likely to get depressed, less likely to lament lost relationships, and less likely to struggle to find a new purpose than extroverts. For extroverts, it all seems harder.

Extroverts' mental health after walking away will require more intentional effort to stay in balance. They especially should pre-plan for a new and meaningful purpose in life. They should come up with a new identity. They should make sure they stay busy and find groups to interact with. Extroverts should prepare for the chance they might become mildly depressed, and understand that it's only a phase. It will pass.

All business owners should work with a financial planner and estate attorney to invest and protect their assets. For some, it will be a challenge to learn how to enjoy and use their newfound wealth. It may take practice. Even if financially set for life, men, especially, may still find it psychologically necessary to generate income outside of their investments because that's how they've measured their worth over their lifetimes. It's how society measures the worth of a man.

Those with generational wealth should work with a wealth manager to protect future generations. *Shirtsleeves to shirtsleeves in three generations* isn't just a pithy saying. It's a reality that takes effort and forethought to avoid. Business owners are accustomed to business missions and values and the importance of culture. With guidance, this can be translated to their families, resulting in a multi-generational legacy. The knowledge that they are caring for their children and grandchildren gives owners tremendous satisfaction and contentment.

Selling a business for the first time is the most important financial decision in a business owner's life. It can and should be an exciting and rewarding adventure. If owners are aware of, and prepare for, the emotional ups and downs of the roller coaster, they will emerge mentally healthier and financially stronger.

I

MOTIVES

The sale of a business is not random or spontaneous. People do not wake up one day and think, *It's time to sell the old business.* It's not like a car or a boat.

The decision to sell is often the result of a build-up. For example, there might be a simple weariness that grows after years in the business. The owner comes to realize it's not as much fun as it once was. Nevertheless, he can remain in that state for a good deal of time, years even. Then, a triggering event, such as a conflict with a key employee or customer, occurs. The owner says *Enough!* and he starts the process to sell the business.

The motive may be internal, as described above, or it might be family-related. It might be health-related. One business owner confessed, "It's one thing if you're a sole proprietor. It's another thing if you have a partner, whoever that partner is. Family? That's a whole other thing. When it's a family business, there's behind-the-scenes family dynamics going on that could impact decision-making. Mine was multigenerational and I'm the oldest. I'm a natural leader and super creative and pretty driving. And I'm the complete opposite of my business partner. I couldn't depend on my family business partner to take over any more of the operation. Matter of fact, I was constantly reassigning her responsibilities to other people because things did not go very well. I didn't see another exit."

It might be the near miss of litigation that could have bankrupted the business owner. In every case, there was some internal or external change that stimulated action. Often, powerful emotions kick into gear surrounding the trigger point.

The Business-Exit Roller Coaster

While it sometimes happens, rarely is the decision to sell a business a mere transaction. Even then, there's a catalyst, such as the owner of local radio frequencies who was money-whipped by a buyer who was assembling a nationwide mobile-phone network. And even though this might have been a simple business transaction to the owner of the radio frequencies, there were still powerful emotions involved. The emotions surrounded the offer and what the sudden wealth could mean for the business owner and his family.

Sometimes the catalyst is an internal clock that the owner is barely conscious of. The clock says, *It's time. Sell it now.* One owner exemplified this. He said, "I think because I did it on my terms, I didn't feel like I better sell this or I may never get any bigger than this, or I need to sell this or I don't feel like I can run it, or something like that. It was very much a 'there's a time for everything' feeling. I was done. Time to sell. So that was kind of the deal. And I'd watched some friends sell too late. They kind of let the company get away from them in some ways, or the industry got away from them. So many business owners neglect the reality that to keep a business alive, there has to be a continued reinvestment in both capital and staying current with the changes in the industry."

One business owner simply changed her outlook and started valuing time more than money. She said, "My parents are part of an investment group that teaches people about creating financial freedom for themselves through alternative investments outside of the stock market. Typically, this is real estate, oil and gas, private lending, and things like that. I started going to these conferences with them and learned about creating financial freedom without trading time for money. It sparked a different mentality. I realized I didn't have to spend the next 25 years working my tail off just to provide for my family. I can actually be smarter and create passive income by selling the business I created and using that as a stepwise building block towards greater wealth without more effort."

Another business owner said that his advancing age prompted him to sell. He said, "I guess I sold because of my age more than anything else. I was ready. I was practicing for 37 years. It was just the right time. I told everybody, every employee, I felt like I won the Super Bowl. I'm on top. I'd like to walk out just that way. And that's what it felt like. People ask me, 'Do you wish you'd have stayed?' No. I love my staff. I love the clients. I miss seeing the people. But there are other things in my life. It was a dream to start a practice, but I didn't want to overstay my welcome. That was my big thing."

"Make sure it's on your timeline," advised a business owner, "not on somebody else's timeline. Everybody gets the calls every week. We're very interested in companies like yours, blah, blah, blah. But if you're not ready, you will essentially give your company away. Get it ready to sell."

Priorities do change with time. Some owners conclude it's time to sell when the business falls in importance. "I had met the love of my life and I had actually moved," said a business owner. "I had moved 45 miles away from my office. I used to live 4.5 miles from my office. Now I was living 45 miles from my office, and I was now working remote for a lot of the time. I only went into the office three days a week. I'd had a personal shift in my life, which I don't really talk about a lot with people as the reason for selling the business."

Business owners should take inventory of their reasons for selling and take more than a few moments to process them. Are the reasons to sell clear enough to motivate the business owner to proceed with the process, and more importantly, to stick to the plan all the way *past* the finish line? A clearly defined reason is critical to staying on target.

As a rule, the business owners who sold their companies fell into two camps: proactive and reactive. The proactive camp took steps to prepare to sell before it was forced on them. They were able to start the process of emotionally separating themselves from their companies. The reactive camp was the opposite. They were not ready when circumstances forced a sale. They weren't mentally prepared. As a result, the emotions surrounding the sale tended to be more traumatic.

If selling a business is a game, then the time leading up to the decision is the pre-game. It's deciding to play and getting mentally ready for the action to come.

1: Investor Return

For companies with funding from outside investors, there is pressure to generate a return on the investment. The intensity of the pressure is a function of the investors' time horizon. The shorter the horizon, the greater the pressure.

If the business is organized as a pass-through for tax purposes, such as an S Corp or an LLC, investors will be taxed on the company's profits. The problem is that some of the profits need to be retained and reinvested for future growth, including capital investment, and simply retaining enough working capital to operate. Outside investors may be sympathetic to the needs of a growing business, but the taxes are still due. Accordingly, the executives are typically expected to at least return enough profits to cover the outsiders' tax liability.

Businesses organized as C Corps are taxed at the corporate level, and outside investors have no tax liability unless a dividend is paid. Then, the taxes are a percentage of the dividend, taxed as ordinary income. This, of course, represents double taxation. The corporation is taxed, and any dividends are taxed at the individual level. For a growing business, it's often preferable to retain all profits to avoid double taxation. This means outside investors receive no return until the business is sold, the executives execute a stock buy-back, or they issue a dividend.

No matter how the business is organized, outside investors will eventually want a return on their money. As time proceeds, the pressure for a return builds, even for long-term investors. This can create a dilemma if the company's value increases to the point where the inside owners are unable or unwilling to raise the funds to buy out the outside investors at a fair market value. Ultimately, this prompts the executives to seek other investors or a sale of the business.

Executives with ownership equity are conflicted, to say the least, even when the ownership share represents majority control. If the owner isn't ready to walk away, giving up control may constitute a sense of inevitable loss that's been described as watching a child move out of the house or a daughter getting married. It may be necessary, but there is still a sense of loss.

Raging against the desire to remain in control is the sense of obligation to the outside investors. In almost all cases, investor funding and other support was considered critical to the growth and success of the enterprise. Thus, the majority owners felt compelled to do what was right, despite personal sacrifice.

"I had a group of people who put up the money for me to start my company," confessed one business owner. "Over time, they began to ask for their investments as they began to look to retirement and, in some cases, the sale of their own companies. I couldn't afford to buy them out at anything close to a fair market value. I needed to bring in other investors. In the end, I would probably have to give up majority control, so I said 'Screw it' and just put the whole business on the market."

Outside or passive investors will eventually ask for a return on their investment, if not a return of their entire investment. If the principals of the business cannot afford to buy out the investors at fair market value, they should consider selling the business.

2: Investment

A business's growth rate is limited by its operating income. If the growth opportunities exceed internal financing, then the options are debt financing, the infusion of additional equity from the owner, or outside investment.

Large corporations can issue their own bonds for debt financing. Small and mid-caps must seek bank financing or private lenders. These may not be attractive or available. If they aren't, the owner is confronted with a choice: Put more personal funds into the business or seek outside investment. In the current environment, outside investment often means giving up majority control.

Many, if not most, business owners tamp down their growth expectations to what can be funded internally, through bank lines of credit or personal investment. Yet some owners are willing to cede control if they see the investment helping them to achieve an attractive and otherwise unattainable vision. In some cases, there's a pressing need to act to avoid an erosion of market share and/or value. The challenge is not keeping up with the Joneses; it's keeping up with the marketplace.

The business owners who sought outside investment to fund strategic shifts or growth tended to make calculated assessments. To them, there really was no choice and no dilemma. The investment was needed to ensure the future success of the enterprise. They felt additional funding was absolutely critical. An example is a software company that was moving to a cloud-based SaaS (software as a service) model. The owner could have funded it, but was unwilling to take the risk. Thus, he sought a partner, which purchased the majority of the shares and provided the funding needed for the strategic shift to occur.

"The reason I sold was kind of interesting," said the software executive. "There's a big changeover in our industry with everything moving to the cloud rather than on-premise or in a local data center. The big thing was to move everything to Amazon Web Services or to Microsoft Azure, to Google, and get out of running it on your own and let them run it for you. We did that to a certain extent. Probably 60% of our business turned into cloud business. But for the rest, it was going to take quite an investment on my part. It pretty much would mean cashing in all the equity I had in the company to totally transform us into a cloud-based company. At that time, I was in my late fifties. I really wasn't too keen on making that investment. So that's when I decided to sell the company."

Another business owner weighed the need for additional investment against the probable delay in his retirement. He said, "I had hit the point where I was at that 50-person threshold where you've got different reporting requirements and EEOC requirements. There's all kinds of other stuff that you have to do. Whether I was right or wrong, I had in my mind that I would have to hire another person just to manage that reporting. And that wouldn't be a minimum-wage person. That would be a pretty smart person to do all of that. And then in order to pay that salary, I would really need to buy a whole other team, so another survey truck and two surveyors and the survey equipment that goes with it, and then the drafter to take care of the work that the surveyors bring in, and then an engineer or two to take care of the engineering that they're going to bring in. I was looking at another million-dollar investment, and my retirement horizon was getting further and further down to the horizon. That may not have been the truth of the matter, but that's what was in my head. That's one of the reasons why I called the broker back and said, I at least need to talk and see what they're thinking and what the options are, and maybe this will get me off of my hump."

Sometimes, the business needs more capital than the business can internally generate. If this is the case, the business owner should either borrow the money, inject equity, or sell all or part of the company to a third party.

3: Family/Partner Buyouts

Very similar to investor-driven sales is the need to buy out a family member or business partner. If the resources available to buy out the owners who want to leave the company are sufficient, and acceptable terms can be reached, there is no need to seek outside funding. When either fails and the resources are insufficient (including raising resources through debt) or terms cannot be reached, the need to seek outside funding becomes apparent.

The advent of private equity has upset the dynamic of internal funding. Private equity has increased market pricing, raising the expectations of owners/partners who want to exit. What was once an acceptable buyout is no longer sufficient. This might mean a sale of the business is now necessitated.

A business owner explained, "My partner wanted to retire, then all of a sudden this out-of-the-blue offer comes in and upsets the apple cart as far as the valuation that we were thinking. I was going to be paying my partner an amount significantly less than the offer from the buyer. This changed everything. We are now looking at quite a bit more money, and how was I going to fund that large of a buyout? So, we went back and forth on the idea of selling to the buyer for a week, just discussing pros and cons of selling. Ultimately, we decided we'd go down the path."

In some cases, it's pure economics. It's one thing to sell a small family business to an ambitious family member, especially when there are few buyers, but when the family business attracts outside investor interest it becomes a very different situation. It may be difficult, if not impossible, to saddle a family member with the burden of buying the business at, or near, the price an outside investor might pay. Taking less than the market price for a family business becomes tricky when there are multiple siblings and only one plans to buy the business.

One business owner intended to sell to a son until he discovered the price his business could command on the open market. He said, "The intention was always to sell it to my oldest son. He worked in the company, and my youngest son and daughter had great careers outside of the family business. I expected I'd have to carry a note and my oldest son would buy me out over time. We approached a consultant to get a valuation. Much to my surprise, I learned that PE would probably be interested in my business at a purchase price way higher than anything I felt comfortable burdening my son with. I mean, he was capable of running the business, but did I really want my son loaded down with 10 million dollars in debt? If I sold to him at a more reasonable price, it wouldn't be fair to my other son and daughter. In the end, we sold to PE."

When a partner or family member with equity wants to exit the business, and the remaining partner or family member lacks the resources or desire to buy the individual's equity or borrow the necessary funds, then the business owner should consider selling all or part of the business. This will become increasingly common as private equity bids up market pricing in some industries.

4: Family Pressure

As business owners age, their adult children can put pressure on them to sell. Whether or not they're in the business, the children's motivation is usually concern for their parents' health and happiness and the stress the business puts on them. In other cases, the kids simply want to see their parents enjoy the fruits of a lifetime of labor.

In some ways, pressure from the kids to sell is similar to the pressure some parents face from their children when they feel it's time to move to assisted living. The parents will put it off as long as possible, while the concern and worry of their children continues to grow.

"My son is involved in real estate and he wanted my daughter to take over running his real estate business," explained one business owner, giving a different motive for pressure from the children. "At the time, she was helping me in the business. So that was his motive for getting me to sell. He wanted to hire my daughter. They had been after me for several years, so when I had a diagnosis with cancer, it became the time to do it."

He continued, "It was family pressure. I enjoyed what I was doing. I liked going to work every day, so that was hard. I guess you are never ready to retire. But, that being said, I have been very busy in the last year. I don't know how I ever had time to work.

"The family pressure was definitely there," he added. "It never got ugly or anything like that; it was just there. I do prison ministry work, and my son is very successful in his real estate ventures. He would say, 'Just close the doors on the business and walk away from it. I will support you.' So, I do have excellent family support."

Business owners should listen to adult children and other family members who, out of concern for their well-being or happiness, encourage them to sell.

5: Marital Strife

Running a business puts stress on a marriage. When spouses work together as a team, both experience the stress of business ownership. Some couples are drawn together by the challenges. In other cases, especially when there are different tolerances for pressure or risk, the business can drive a couple apart.

When only one spouse works in the business, it can seem to the one who isn't involved that the other has a mistress (which is exactly how some business owners described their companies).

A software executive recalled how he returned home from a business trip to find his wife and two young children waiting for him. The wife was dressed to go out. She passed the kids to him and left. Her husband said it became apparent to him that he could remain an entrepreneur or he could remain married. "I honor my contractual relationship with my wife, but also my covenant relationship with my wife. I was born and raised as a Boy Scout by Boy Scouts... You know, trustworthy, loyal, helpful, friendly, all those things. I try to be those things and live those things. I saw that I had a mistress in a business. I was loving my business more than I was loving my family. This is not healthy. Selling the company was just the right thing to do for lots and lots and lots of reasons. It was just the right thing to do for my family. It was the right thing to do for my customers. It wouldn't have done any good for me to go through a divorce. It wouldn't have done my employees any good. It would not have done any good for anybody except for my lawyers."

He sold his business for his marriage and his family. He considered it a price worth paying, noting, "We've been married for 40 years and have great relationships with our two kids. That's worth it, right? To me, that's worth it."

Business ownership can take a toll on a marriage when the business becomes a "mistress." If the pressure is too great, the owner may need to sell the business to save the marriage.

6: Health

Eventually, everyone exits. Some exit by walking out on their own two feet. Some exit horizontally. No one operates a business forever. Everyone is mortal. Everyone ages. As people age, health issues become more frequent. For many business owners, declining health is the driving force to sell the business. With a slow decline, the owner can go through an orderly process. In dire situations, the health issue can be severe enough that the sale of the business must be made in haste.

One middle-aged business owner was motivated to sell after his wife asked him to give her just ten more years. Ten more years was in doubt. In reality, five years seemed unlikely. He decided to sell the business and focus on life, longevity, and health. The business was profitable, growing, and he enjoyed running it, but decided lifestyle changes necessitated a sale.

"You're so used to the stress and so used to being wound up, you kid yourself," he recalled. "I was five-foot-nine and 255 pounds. I'd go to sleep and I was so heavy that my shoulder would cause my arm to fall asleep because there was too much weight on my shoulder. Little cues like that made me look at another way of doing things. Was I going to die if I did not change? Yes! So I think overall health was why I sold."

All business owners reported that, post-transaction, they felt healthier, with less stress, less worry, and less running high-speed, non-stop, seven days a week. One owner reported, "It felt as if the busier we were, the better we were. We just lived for stress. Now we are healthier. We have to be healthier. The only stress I have now is whether or not the hardware store will be open early enough for me to get my handyman projects together. That's the only thing I have to worry about."

Another owner claimed selling his business "relieved me of stress that would have killed me probably within the next year. I'm convinced I would have had a health episode. I've never been on blood pressure meds, never been on cholesterol meds. I'm 10 pounds or 15 pounds overweight at the moment. It's not like I'm a classic case for a heart attack. My doctor asked, 'What're you doing? What are you going through?' I described it all. He said, 'Dude, this is all stress.'"

"I was diagnosed with Crohn's disease," said another business owner. "It's bad enough I'm going to lose part of my intestines at some point. I'm going to have this forever. There's no cure. It's the medium-to-severe level of this disease. It shook me enough to say, 'Alright, you need to go and live.' That was kind of my wake-up call that I needed to be more intentional about my life. And that included not working until I was 60."

Business ownership is stressful, so stressful that, in some cases, it impacts the health of the owner. Some business owners should sell their companies to live longer, healthier lives.

7: Death

The death of a principal can result in the motivation, if not outright need, to sell. The majority of these cases surround a partnership where one of the partners cannot continue or where a surviving spouse may not feel comfortable running the business alone.

When a partner passes away, the surviving partner may not feel able to take over. For example, the partners might be the classic Mr. Inside and Mr. Outside. Each needs the other and may not want to continue if forced to cover both roles or if unable to find an acceptable replacement for the deceased partner.

In other cases, the deceased partner's spouse might want to cash out. If the remaining partner is unwilling or unable to buy out the spouse at fair market value and the spouse will not accept being paid over time, the sale of the business may be forced.

When a spouse is the primary manager of the operation, the survivor may not feel capable or have the inclination to run the business alone. The spouse will often step up in the short term, but this is extremely challenging. While working through the grief and life adjustment that result from the loss of a life partner, the spouse must also lead the organization and possibly assume unfamiliar duties.

A widowed business owner explained how she and her husband had divided responsibilities. "We were operating a drone-service provider business. We ran and built the business together, but the technical side was never my wheelhouse. My husband was the technical expert. He got licensed as a private pilot. He did all the FAA materials, regulations. I was the business side. I would do payroll for our pilots. I would do the contracting. I managed the accounting software and everything."

Despite this, she felt ill-equipped to take on her husband's responsibilities after he passed away. "I was left with this company that I'd built side-by-side with my husband, but I didn't have my drone pilot's license. I didn't know all the latest FAA regulations. I had no idea how to vet pilots or anything. I was not the technical expert."

Beyond the challenges of the business, she had to deal with the trauma that accompanies the unexpected loss of a spouse. "I was wrecked. My brain did not work for two years. Grief will jack you up. My brain simply did not work. I had friends living with me 24/7 for the first three weeks because I could barely function."

She realized she needed to sell. "In the midst of my grief I'm thinking, *How am I going to keep this business alive?* I realized I'm going to have to sell before it is totally flatlined. I thought, *If I don't sell this business fast it's going to look like it's worth nothing.*"

The owner knew she needed help selling the company, but didn't know whom to trust or how to find a broker. She said, "I actually ended up getting a letter in the mail. As widows or anybody who's lost a loved one, you'll start to get a whole bunch of letters of crazy stuff. One of them was a picture of a business broker with his wife and kids at the bottom. In his letter, he talked about his family. He was a strong Christian and believed in building relationships first. He wrote that if he could help, he would. I put that letter on the kitchen counter for a week or two. Finally, I just felt this nudge to just give him a call."

It may not be the death of a spouse or partner that provides the impetus to sell a business. Another owner described how the loss of his father moved him to begin the process of finding a buyer for his business. He said, "My dad passed away about three years ago. As most people in these family businesses would say, he was a mentor to me. Even post-retirement, he was in the office every day. It felt different when he wasn't there, not in the sense that I didn't want to work or didn't want to run the business. It just… It accelerated my drive to find a buyer and find something that I could live with."

The death of a spouse or key business partner can necessitate the sale of a business. Survivors should be prepared to sell when their skill set is insufficient or the grief is overwhelming.

8: Burnout

Some people burn out. Running a business involves risk and responsibility. Different people have different levels of tolerance for the pressure that comes from meeting a payroll every week or managing a workforce that may only be marginally engaged. It wears.

The result is that some business owners reach a point where they've just had *enough*. They become open to the constant stream of search equity and private equity inquiries.

There's a danger that a burnt-out business owner might leap at one of the inquiries without fully understanding the market or the fair market value of the business. Maybe he gets a good offer. Maybe he doesn't. Either way, he doesn't know.

One business owner, who recognized and admitted being burnt out, talked about how he gradually came to recognize it was time to walk away. First, he recognized he could sell his business. Second, he started thinking about life after the business. Finally, he reached a tipping point.

He said, "I listened to an industry consultant who got in my head about having a business that I would be able to sell. I always admired a lot of my customers who seemed to appear to retire comfortably, travel, and enjoy life. That was always in the back of my mind, retiring whenever it was convenient. Then there was a point where I was tired of training people. I didn't want to go through another training period for another five, six years.

"I started the business in my garage when I was 23. I did not go to college. I made up for that by working long hours. The business was what I did, seven days a week, for 25 years. I put a daughter through college and my wife and I enjoyed a comfortable lifestyle, but I was no longer happy. The thrill of the business was gone and I felt like I was starting to go through the motions. The business was fine. I just no longer found satisfaction in it. I guess you could say I was burned out."

Another business owner said, "After 38 years I was a little burned out. My wife and I had the chance to travel around the world and do amazing things because we found a GM who could manage the business. In the end, the GM declared he was either going to buy the business or leave. So, you could say both burnout and pressure from an employee to buy the business were the reasons to sell."

Jacob and Michel

Longevity can also lead to burnout. A business owner who took over his father's business said, "My father had me and my brother working in the business by the time we turned 14. So, at 50, you could say we have been involved with the business for a long time and, after 35 years of doing the same thing, burnout sets in. It quickly turned from not really enjoying the daily grind to dreading it. Burnout is a big reason why we sold the business."

While burnout may not have been a motive to sell for one business owner, it was nevertheless present. He said, "I never realized how burnt out I was until after the transaction closed." The seller, who stayed on post-transaction to achieve an earnout, explained, "Little things started to bother me that never bothered me before. Silly things like employees calling in sick."

Several business owners clearly described being burnt out, though they didn't actually use the term. There is something in the entrepreneurial DNA that won't allow them to claim burnout, even if they recognize it. For example, one business owner said, "Sometimes there comes a time when you talk about what the next chapter is. It was two years ago for me. I was 66 years old. I wondered, were the best days in front of me or the best days behind me? What did I see in front of me? Did I see going into the office and dealing with all of the HR issues, Walmart contracts, suppliers who don't deliver, doing wire transfers every week, and teaching people how to sell the same product I've been selling for 40 years? I was just tired."

The husband in a couple-run business talked about the stress, but avoided the claim of burnout. "We could see we had a big organization and it was us seeing 120 customers a week. From the time you got there in the morning until the time you left at seven or eight in the evening, it was non-stop. Stress was just off the charts."

Another business owner talked about how the pressure built over time. He described a situation where an employee was stealing from his customers. He said, "I'll tell you, that was stressful for me. I was the 100% shareholder of a closely held business. I'm out of town at a softball tournament with my daughter when I get a call from a county detective. He asked if a certain employee worked for me and I said yes.

"The detective said, 'Well, he has been systematically stealing jewelry from your customers' homes for the last year.' I asked, 'What can I do?' He said he'd handle it. The employee was fencing the stuff through this pawn shop. We were able to recover 90% of it. These were Naval Academy class rings. These were Holocaust rings. These were things where this idiot 26-year-old kid had no idea of their worth. The cops came and arrested him. He admitted to all of it. The guy was such a sociopath. I paid restitution back to his victims. It was $14,800, because what I couldn't have was bad press. When you're the 100% shareholder and don't have a board, you get so sick."

He concluded, "The term I would use is it's *cumulative*. It's like Lego blocks. You know, it weighs."

Employee problems seem to be a frequent cause of burnout. One owner noted, "The types of people that we typically have to employ to work in sign companies are a challenge. It's attitudes. It's very traditional for them to have lots of addictions. It's rare to find someone who hasn't been to jail, been on drugs, or an alcoholic."

> ***Business owners consider burnout a weakness, so they won't name it even though they experience the symptoms. Business owners should recognize burnout and consider selling their companies if it begins to significantly impact performance.***

Jacob and Michel

9: Risk Avoidance

Business owners are, by nature, risk-tolerant. Risk is part and parcel of business ownership, and business owners tend to handle greater levels of risk than the average person. However, over time, the risk will build as the company grows and there is more to lose. At some point, business owners may decide it's time to take chips off the table rather than risk more rounds in the game.

"I was tired of hanging it out there every day," confessed one owner. "There's a lot of risk. I remember the times that I would start to think about some risky situation, someone getting injured or, heaven forbid, a death. I used to worry about somebody getting killed on a job. It happens. I would worry about the risk. There was a lot of risk I took and a lot of chances that could have turned south on me. You carry insurance to offset that risk, but it's never 100%."

Business risk takes many forms. The universal risk is simply the potential loss of equity or reduction in value due to poor performance. This motivates some, but the bigger risk is due to external factors that are beyond the business owner's control.

The litigious nature of today's society drives some to exit. If a business owner has endured a round or two of litigation, he might punt. Owners punt even if successful in court because they can envision losing everything due to the emotional judgment of a jury made up of incompetents and the ignorant. *Get out now,* they reason.

"I had fears about the lawsuit I went through," one owner said. "It went to jury trial. It was a three-month trial. At the closing statements, the prosecution said, 'We're looking to get 10 million dollars for this lawsuit.' We didn't do anything wrong. It was just a full money-grab. If I would have approached the situation with confidence and just said, *Everything's going to be fine. Even if I lose everything, I'm still going to be fine,* then I probably would have been okay mentally. It boils down to fear. Fear just eroded my confidence. It took over."

Another risk is running afoul of an EEOC complaint or other government rule or regulation. The business owners expressing this concern tended to operate in more regulated states and believed right and wrong had little to do with the outcome of a case. If an employee filed an EEOC complaint due to a perceived or fabricated grievance, the owners felt like they were assumed guilty until they could prove

45

their innocence. The same owner quoted above said, "There was an employment lawsuit as well. It's just another thing where the odds are stacked against you."

Another owner said, "There's a lot of pressure if you get hit with a lawsuit. Those things are a big drain. We had a couple. Very rarely was it our fault, but we have a couple blunders that we had to step up and take care of."

Beyond the risk of torts is the personal guarantees small business owners are compelled to sign. For example, when a small business leases commercial real estate, the lease carries the owner's personal guarantee. If the business borrows money, it likewise carries the owner's personal guarantee. This is true whether it's to purchase real estate, capital equipment, vehicles, inventory, or a line of credit. Business debt obligates the business owner personally. If the business cannot repay the debt or meet a lease obligation, the owner is personally liable. It's another factor prompting some owners to sell.

"My business was heavily reliant upon debt," noted a business owner. "At the time of the sale, I was personally guaranteeing over 20 million dollars in bank loans. So, for me, the deal was not all about the purchase price, but rather, could I live comfortably after the debt was paid off? In the end, the buyer offered enough so that I could pay off the debt and also feel I had enough left over to live comfortably. What I did not realize was the sense of relief that came from no longer living underneath the pressure of guaranteeing so much debt."

An irony about risk is that the process of selling the business can be the most risk-laden time of ownership. Those who tried to navigate the sale on their own, without professional guidance, encountered exponentially greater risk, though many were unaware of it. The risk took the form of rookie mistakes. One business owner recognized this and said, "I went under an LOI three times. Every time the deal fell apart. It fell apart for different reasons each time. Finally, I said, *Screw it; this is killing me.* I interviewed a bunch of investment banks and picked one. These guys do this all of the time, so they kept the deal on track, kept me from making unforced errors, and ultimately got me more money."

Business ownership requires risk tolerance. The acceptance of risk is a key difference between entrepreneurs and employees. When the risk becomes too much for a business owner, especially after the business has become successful (i.e., saleable), the owner should consider selling the company.

10: Changing Business Environment

Some owners look at the business horizon and see evolving technology, increasing government regulations, and other structural changes that will make business more challenging and possibly make it difficult to maintain current profit margins going forward. These owners chose to exit while they can still take advantage of the higher margins and EBITDA (earnings before interest, taxes, depreciation, and amortization) of the current environment.

In addition, if business owners anticipate increases in the capital gains tax due to political changes at the national or state/provincial level, they might act to take advantage of the more favorable, current tax structure, even if they aren't otherwise ready to sell. They reason that the effort required to increase EBITDA stands to be wiped out by a changing tax structure. So, they reason, why not cash out now?

The owner of an engineering firm illustrates this. He said, "Why I sold? I needed a retirement. I didn't want to work for the rest of my life, so I needed some way to exit. There was a competitor, a strategic, and a private equity group that were trying to roll up a bunch of design companies. I had three potential offers, three suitors when I was looking. The timing of the decision was purely based on the election in 2020. And so, regardless of which politics you believe in, every single financial guy in the world said that capital gains was going to go up. That was a guarantee when Biden took office. Now, it didn't take place because he's been doing other crap. But every advisor thought they would go up. I would have been devastated if someone took double the taxes out, if they raised capital gains from 20% to 51% or whatever. On Biden's website, he said 51.3%."

Of course, not all changes are the result of government action. The introduction of private equity has affected many industries. Depending on the stage of consolidation, business owners may look on the current time to be an excellent one to exit and fear that, due to their size, financial might, employee benefits, buying power, or other factors, private equity-absorbed companies will be harder to compete with. They might also fear that private equity will soon run its course in their industry so they should grab the brass ring while they can.

"In pharmacy and medicine in general, there is a consolidation," said a business owner. "There's just basically going to be one or two pharmacies, and in probably ten years, CVS or Walgreens. So, the two big giants, and that's not even big enough in healthcare. They're combining with insurance companies, with the mail-order pharmacies, the payers, administrators, they're all combining."

He continued, "There's always changes, and now they've always talked about technology and everybody being replaced by kiosks and robots. It's possible, because if you look at what can happen, you can have vending machines, basically in doctor's offices, act as pharmacies. So, the value of the pharmacy was becoming less and less, just like medical practices. You can't sell a medical practice. You used to be able to. Now you can't, because they're not worth anything."

Another owner talked about changing technology. He noted, "Technology is going to pass all of us by. This world is technologically going to go past 60-year-old guys pretty fast. Everything is all data. The marketing is technology, Google Analytics, and all that crap. I get most of it and I learn a lot, but I feel like that's a 30-year-old game, Gen Z. And then all the other BS, between politics and regulations. Those were a bunch of the reasons. I was ready."

Another business owner echoed the concerns about changes in technology. He said, "I felt we were limited in our ability to incorporate new technology into the business in the form of software systems, operational systems, things of that nature. That's the reason why I sold the company."

While not encountered in the research conducted for this book, the impact of artificial intelligence may prompt some business owners to exit. These are owners who do not want to embrace AI, while simultaneously fearing that businesses will need to master it to succeed.

The pace of technology and requirements to keep up with it is another aspect of a changing industry that factors in the decision of business owners to sell. The more hands-on the owner is, the greater the challenge from changing technology appears to be. "Our industry changes every day," noted a business owner. "If we go on vacation for a week or two, you come back and what's happened? Everything has just evolved. Lightning changes. What floated our boat at our automotive shop was diagnostics. We had every diagnostic tool known to man. We sent all of our team to all of the schools. Anybody can screw in a spark plug, anybody can throw a set of brake pads on a car, but can you fix the damn car? That was what our pride and joy was, fixing cars. To stay on top of our industry, we were always in school, always. But as we aged, it got harder and harder to stay on the cutting edge."

Industry structures, regulations, taxes, and the external business environment can change over time. Technology, especially artificial intelligence, is in constant flux. Business owners may consider selling when facing an uncertain or perceived unattractive future.

11: Fear

Beyond the potential of lawsuits, tax changes, industry shifts, and other factors, there is a general fear that affects some business owners. While the difference is subtle, fear is not the same as risk. As mentioned, business owners tend to be more risk-tolerant than the average person; if they weren't, they would never own companies. However, over time, the owner's awareness and fear of the things that can go wrong, ranging from employee issues to business fraud to accidents involving company vehicles to the ominous weight of business debt to making a tax mistake, begin to take a toll.

The fear becomes a constant nagging voice, a worry at the pit of the stomach. It can become too much for some people and they begin to see the business as a burden.

A proverb states, "Don't put all of your eggs in one basket." Business owners may have heard it growing up. Once they became business owners, they lived it. All of a business owner's eggs tend to be in the basket known as *the business*. Most of an owner's net worth is tied up in the business. This makes the consequences of failure more severe, which raises risks and increases fear.

One owner talked about the fear. "It's about security for the family, right? I'm now 45. My wife and I have three children. Before selling, all I ever worried about is what happens if I get hit by a bus? So, selling the business to me was having a paid-off house, having college paid, and all of the things that are most important. So, if I get hit by a bus tomorrow, my wife's not in bad shape, my kids are not in bad shape. I know the family's taken care of. That was first and foremost."

It was more than just security for the business owner. It was also the absence of fear. He continued, "I'd go to bed at 10:00 p.m., I'd be up by 1:30 a.m. because everything weighs on you. There'd be times my wife would call me at 3:00 a.m. in the morning and ask, 'Where are you?' I drove to the office because I couldn't sleep. I'm just getting things done. I was up to 304 pounds at the time. I was a big boy. I'd never been that big in my life. My health was a wreck."

Risk levels are naturally higher for some businesses than others. An agricultural business owner said, "Mother Nature is your partner. Mother Nature is not always predictable. She's not really nice, and it's a lot of tension. A lot of stress."

It should be no surprise that a sale brings relief. This was stressed repeatedly by business owners. Once the transaction closed, the fear was removed.

"When I closed the sale," said one business owner, "I would say I felt more relief than anything else. I don't have the pressure weighing on me anymore. Because there's always a pressure when you own the business. You've got 40, 50 mouths, families, that you've got to feed. There's always that pressure. Even when I was down working two days a week, I still kind of felt the pressure because I was still in that mindset. Now I don't have that pressure. So there's relief."

"It was just such a relief," said another owner. "It was the relief of not having to run the practice, a relief that the money's in the bank. It was just such a sense of relief."

"The emotion I felt when I sold was relief. The one thing that scares me in business is the treasury department, the IRS. I do all my taxes through automatic payments. Everything's done. If you get sideways with the IRS, they have a trust fund recovery act where they come after you personally. It's not a corporate deal."

As a business becomes successful, some business owners begin to fear everything that can go wrong. When the fear becomes too great to bear, the business owner should consider selling.

Jacob and Michel

12: Retirement

Every business owner will exit the business one day. As noted earlier, some walk away vertically while others exit horizontally. For those who choose to leave on two feet and retire, they can shut the business down, sell to family or employees, or find a third party. Retirement-driven sales tend to be protracted, with the owner trying to find the optimal way to turn the business over to someone who will be able to buy him out. When this involves sales to family or employees, the process can take years.

Business owners who are planning retirement should start thinking about the sale of the business well in advance (i.e., *years* in advance). Not only can the process take time, certain buyers will expect the seller to stay on for up to two years before transitioning out. While there is no standard transition period, having the flexibility to remain active for a period of time can be the difference between selling the business and giving it away. Additionally, those who remained with the business for a transitional period generally had an easier adjustment into retirement than those who left the day after close.

A key factor is determining whether the money from the sale is sufficient to retire. Few people take as analytic an approach as one buyer did. He said, "I did the math. I looked at what our profits were and what our EBITDA was and I looked at the multiples buyers were paying. Then I did the math backwards on what my wife and I needed to live on comfortably without touching the principal and we hit that number. We easily hit that number. So that was that. It was an unemotional decision. It was strictly business."

Planning for retirement is tricky. Many of the people interviewed avoided the term, but instead treated the sale of their business as closing one chapter of their life before opening another. They didn't see life after a business transaction as a shift from high to low gear, but rather a time in life to enjoy the fruits of their labor and the risks they undertook. Hopefully, they will enjoy the added cash and absence of the stress of business ownership.

One business owner was 60 years old when he sold his company. He said, "I worked 30 years on my business and grew it from a garage startup into over 75 employees and two locations. During all of that time, I never once took more than a long-weekend and only once, on my honeymoon, did I take a full week off. Even when off, I was never really off. Calls, emails, texts and the middle-of-the-night emergencies were common, a way of life! I sacrificed for all those years and, although I don't like to call it being retired, today I do what I want, when I want. For the first time ever, my wife and I just took a three-week vacation to Europe."

Another simply said, "I was getting older. I was wanting to travel more and take advantage of retirement."

If the leadership team of a company is getting long in the tooth and likely to retire themselves, business owners might decide to sell rather than delay their own retirement while hiring and developing a new team. One said, "The three of us who ran the business were all in our 60s, so I was going to have to replace the whole management team. I was either gonna do it now before my managers retire or I was going to have to rebuild the management team and it's another five to six years before it's ready to sell."

A common reason to sell a business is the simplest: Business owners who want to retire should sell their companies.

Jacob and Michel

13: Money

Some owners have no intention to sell but are approached by someone with a huge pile of cash and other incentives that appear too good to pass up. They get money whipped. The owner cannot believe what someone is offering. Greed often takes root and they race to complete the transaction before the buyer realizes what he's doing.

Business owners who started with little seem more prone to becoming money whipped. They are offered more money than they ever imagined. The temptation is irresistible. A business owner said, "This guy walks into my office and he says, 'I want to buy your communications network.' I look him in the face. I remember in my head saying, you son-of-a-bitch, you just can't walk in here and say you want to buy my network! But I said, 'Well, it's not for sale.' And he looked at me and smiled and says, 'You don't know what I'm offering.'"

Ultimately, he took the offer. He said, "My take on it was 1.5 million dollars. Now, I had partners. I think the total amount was six million dollars. Remember where I came from. My daddy was a TV repairman. Growing up, we had nothing."

Getting money whipped sounds like a dream, but it also involves a single buyer. Is the buyer offering market price for the business? The owner likely doesn't know. This is akin to someone knocking on a homeowner's door one afternoon and offering the homeowner more than he ever dreamed to buy his house. It might be a good deal, but it might also be 20% below market. The homeowner doesn't know.

One owner who got money whipped discussed the process. He said, "We went from two million dollars to five million dollars over 18 months, two years. I got a message one day on LinkedIn asking me if I was interested in acquisition. I said no, but I'd heard about this thing called a discovery call, and thought it'd be fun to do that. So, I ended up taking a discovery call because I'm curious. They put me in touch with the buyer. He started throwing around multiples. And I thought, wow!

"I went to my partner and said, 'I just had the weirdest call of my life, and I feel like I should tell you about this.' He said, 'That's intriguing.' We talked to our wives and kids. It was out of the blue, answering a random message on LinkedIn."

Next, he said, "I talked to the former owner of a business the buyer already bought. The buyer asked if we were interested. I said sure. So, they sent me an NDA (non-disclosure agreement) and we started doing the dance. They made an offer. I said no because I had a great business plan, a great vision, and I knew where I was going. But the buyer was willing to pay more. He really wanted the business. The money was just too good. We took it."

If an owner finds himself getting money whipped and feels pressed to make a deal, it's a good idea to take a breath. Rarely is the urgency real. There is time to reach out to an M&A advisor for a gut check. Is this a good deal or not? If a buyer is pressing, is he pressing because he's trying to buy cheap before other buyers enter the picture?

An M&A advisor remarked that owners who get a surprise offer "seek a quick piece of bullshit advice and base their life's most significant financial decision on a conversation at a trade show. These [money-whipped] deals tend to occur without the seller having a lot of advice."

Whether the actual deal is good or not, money whipped business owners usually feel happy with their offers. "I got one of these blind emails from a private equity company," said another business owner. "I said, let me respond to them. We just couldn't say no to the money. It was just a hard thing to do. We're at the top of the bell curve of the valuations. We know that the buying frenzy's not going to last. Once that balloon pops, we would probably have a 10- to 15-year wait period. At the time, I was just 40. I said, I don't want to be in my sixties trying to sell this thing. So, I figured I'd cash in now."

> **Business owners can get "money whipped" by buyers who approach them out of the blue with an offer. Business owners should be careful about unsolicited offers that may or may not represent fair market value.**

14: Insufficient Motives

While the research for this book focused on business owners who sold their companies, there were interviews with owners who decided *not* to sell, at least not yet. In some industries there is pressure from private equity and peers to sell. Yet this is an individual choice. An owner who's not ready to sell today can always sell tomorrow.

When owners decide not to sell, it's usually because the business is more of a lifestyle business, is too small to generate much value in a sale, is extremely profitable, or the owner is not at the point in his life where he wants to sell.

If the owner structures the business properly so that he is not necessary for the day-to-day operations, there might be little reason to sell if the business is generating a reasonable income stream.

Running a small business gives many owners purpose and a reason to get up in the morning. While business owners should consider leaving enough time to explore all that life has to offer beyond that of the day-to-day operations of the business, there are some who *only* want to run their businesses until the day arrives when it's no longer possible. Selling a business is not for them.

For a happy business owner, getting money whipped can make it tempting to sell. One described how he received progressively higher offers, but elected to continue his ownership. He said, "In the first serious conversation I had with a buyer, I said I wouldn't do it for less than four million dollars. I thought if I had four million dollars, that'd be pretty cool. A couple years later I was approached again. This time I was looking at an offer of six million dollars. I didn't want to do it. When it happened a third time, it got closer to 12 million dollars."

At the 12-million-dollar value, the owner was tempted, but took a logical view and concluded he shouldn't sell. He said, "My wife and I calculated what it takes for us to enjoy the life we live. It's not much. We're debt-free and can live on 120 grand a year, which is not a lot of money. I don't owe anything and I don't have investors. So, even if the business has ups and downs, it doesn't fundamentally matter. The return from my investments outpaces our spending. I reinvest the profits back into the business or invest them in the stock market. And at this point, the business is just a cash cow. It's just a literal cash cow. I'm financially independent without selling, so why sell?"

Another owner with no intention to sell said, "If I had to go in at 5:00 a.m. in the morning, I would, but I haven't had to do that in five years. Both my wife and I are God-fearing people, and He has helped us out tremendously. So, sell the business? If I wanted, I could do that tomorrow. A local competitor's dying for my company. But if we sold, what do we do with the money? My wife is out with her horse right now. I play my golf. I ride my motorcycle. I can go to the office when I want, when I please."

He then highlighted when he might sell, saying, "My only fear is leaving a company to my wife, and she has to deal with it when I'm gone. That's my biggest fear. And who knows? I might outlive her. I don't think so. But then, what if I did outlive her and I'm stuck with this mess when I'm 78 or something? Then I probably would sell it."

"What makes you happy?" he asked. "I think that's the biggest thing. What makes you happy? Are you happy with your business? If you're happy, why are you getting rid of it? You got something that'll make you happier?"

The business owner might have a different take if his children were interested in his business. He said, "I got four boys. And none of them had any interest in buying the company."

"I have not sold my business," another owner reported. "I enjoy coming into the office; it gives me something to do. The few employees that I have are all long-term and I can rely on them to do what needs to be done. I can't imagine life where I didn't have something to do every day. Is there anything wrong with that?"

A buyer said there are times he would advise a business owner to wait before selling. He said, "Sometimes I literally just tell them, 'Hey, you're not ready to sell this business. You need to keep doing what you're doing until you get in a different mindset.'"

While there's nothing wrong with someone owning and operating a business until the day he dies, if that's his choice, it's not acceptable to leave a mess for his spouse, family members, customers and employees. Electing not to sell relieves the owner of the hassle of going through the sales process. It also relieves the owner of that uneasy transition period of finding other things to do once he's no longer running the business. It should *not* relieve him of the need to plan for the inevitable for his family's sake.

For everything there is a season and sometimes it's not the season to sell … yet. A business owner said, "It's a total dichotomy. The business has tons of headaches, but it has more joy than headaches and I don't want to do anything else because it's not that season in my life. When the kids are gone and in college, it'll get real interesting. The energy that I pour into family will go into the business."

Some decide against selling out of a commitment to their employees. They've built a culture that would likely fall apart under different ownership. "I have five employees over 25 years," boasted a business owner. "It's unheard of in this business. I feel a responsibility towards them. They don't work Saturdays. If one of them wants to take an extra two days off, like on Labor Day or whatever day, then he gets it and he still gets paid. He still gets paid if he wants a week off in the summer. If he tells me what week, far enough in advance, he's going to get that week off to go to the beach or wherever. I knew my biggest competitors (who would like to buy my company) require people to work every Saturday. You can't live your life working like that. I actually personally feel that I would be throwing my employees under the bus if I sold. Their quality of life would suffer, even though they're working for a big giant company."

For some business owners, the best decision is NOT selling. If a business produces a good income, is unlikely to generate a large enough sale price to replace the income, and the owner enjoys running the company, he should not feel pressure to sell.

II

GETTING TO THE LOI

Taking a business to market is when the game begins. It's the biggest game of a lifetime because selling a business is likely the largest financial transaction in a business owner's life. It is certainly larger than selling a house. Yet many business owners, who would never consider selling a house without a real estate agent, take a do-it-yourself approach to selling their businesses. Some may have the business acumen and market knowledge to pull this off. Most do not.

In the chapter on being money whipped, selling a business based on a perceived large offer was described as being similar to selling a home to a buyer who knocks on a homeowner's door out of the blue. To continue with the real estate analogy, business owners who sell their companies on their own are like homeowners who put a for-sale-by-owner sign in the front yard hoping the right buyer drives down their street. Maybe he will, but it's more likely he'll never travel by the property. This is why most people use real estate agents who can present a property to many more prospective buyers than any individual does.

Using a real estate agent does involve paying a commission on the sale, but that commission buys well-informed suggestions that can improve the price and reduce the time to sell the property, guidance on the market price, exposure of the property to many more potential buyers, an intermediary between the homeowner and the buyer, the counsel of experience regarding the offer, and help ensuring that the terms of the deal are standard and fair. Most homeowners use real estate agents because they believe the value delivered is worth the commission. Moreover, the price premium received from using a real estate agent versus a for-sale-by-owner approach almost always exceeds the commission.

A business sale is often a once-in-a-lifetime transaction for sellers. Buyers, on the other hand, tend to buy many businesses over time. This is especially true of private equity buyers. Without an intermediary with experience in a business owner's market, the owner is operating at an information and experience deficit when selling by himself.

The owner of an air conditioning company discussed how an M&A advisor warned him off of trying to sell his business by himself. He recalled, "Here's what he said. 'You're a salesman, you sell air conditioners every day of your life. You sold millions of dollars' worth of air conditioners. How many air conditioning companies have you sold?' I said, 'None.' The advisor said, 'Well, then, do you want to have an amateur like you or would you like to have a professional who has bought and sold companies, many, many of them? Which would you rather have? Because the same thing goes with a surgery on your eyeball. Would you want to do it? Here's your scalpel. Would you like to have a professional do it?' And I said, 'Boy, I'm an idiot. Of course I can't sell my own company.'"

The owner continued, talking about how the M&A advisor counseled him to spiff up his building, much like a real estate agent might suggest painting over an acid-green wall. He said, "I can't evaluate it, my business. I can't see it. The most important thing he did is walk in with an external viewpoint and say, 'You can't have that anymore.' He didn't like my personal office decorations. He walked into my warehouse and said, 'What's that? And that and that? That laminator and this, what are all these things? Get them out of here. They're not part of the business. Make this look like an air conditioning company. Nothing but an air conditioning company. And make it look like it's run by a businessman and not a hobby horse.'"

Sellers always have choices in the sale of a business. When dealing with only one prospective buyer, the choice appears binary: to sell or not to sell. In truth, business owners should always bear in mind that there will be other buyers if the current one doesn't work out.

"We were negotiating with a private equity firm on our own," explained one seller. "They'd bought a friend's company and made what seemed like a reasonable offer. My partner and I went to their offices to sign the letter of intent, but paused when we looked over the term sheet. It wasn't what we talked about. The private equity guy started to give us all kinds of double-talk. We walked. A year later we went to market with an investment bank. It took another year to market and sell the company, but we ended up with twice the multiple and because we had grown our revenue, our EBITDA had also doubled. So, we got four times what we were willing to sell for to the PE guy."

That seller was fortunate. If he had sold to the private equity company, he would have left a lot of money on the table. He was also fortunate that he caught the private equity firm's attempt to change the terms. When he went to market later, he used an investment bank and had a choice of buyers.

Using an investment bank, mergers & acquisitions advisor, broker, or other intermediary usually results in competing offers, reassuring the seller of a fair market price. It also strengthens the seller's negotiating position since there are back-ups should the first buyer fall through.

In the negotiation process, business owners should remember that, until the letter of intent is signed, everything is negotiable. This includes price, equity rolls, noncompetes, salary, bonuses, and other perks if the owner stays on. For example, several sellers negotiated for the buyer to pay personal car payments, insurance, maintenance, gas, and all other related expenses. Others used the moment to clarify specific personal items that were not to be part of the transaction, despite being held with the business and, in some cases, actually used by the business.

High stakes mean high stress. The numbers being kicked around can make a business owner's head swim. One of the key roles for a seller's agent is to help the seller keep emotions in check. The agent operates like ballast to stabilize the owner's emotional swings. "It's 9:00 at night and I get a call from a seller having an emotional meltdown," said an M&A advisor. "Part of my role is to keep them on course through the emotional swings, which are inevitable."

With smaller deals, up until the moment of the sale it's normal for the business owner to ask himself if he's doing the right thing. Even owners who sold multigeneration businesses when there wasn't a next generation to step in, often wondered if the move was right.

A buyer discussed how he tried to help his acquisition targets think through whether selling was the right move. He said, "I always go through it with sellers. If you don't want to think about the risk of owning your business going forward and the risk that you might have a safety problem that would put you out of business, or you might have a major account leave you, that could take all of your profitability away at the multiples that most companies sell at, you may just want to keep it and just keep milking it each year."

Then he would flip the argument. "But the problem is, the price to stay continues to escalate. So does the cost of safety practices, the cost of proper operations, the cost of proper equipment, the cost of insurance, everything keeps going up. There's a lot of investment. There's a huge amount of risk. And frankly, COVID really exposed the amount of risk we have, because I never even dreamed how much risk we had. When COVID hit, my customers shut down. They were closed."

Selling a business can be fun. For some business owners, it's a new experience and, with proper guidance and support, the uncertainty is less daunting. One said, "As stressful as it was and the ups and downs and emotional roller coaster that it is, it was a blast because I was learning the whole time. I was learning something I never knew anything about. So I love that part of it."

15: Uncertainty

Selling a business is a new journey and new territory for most business owners. The stakes are high. The uncertainty can seem overwhelming. And why not? It's only natural that the unknowns and uncertainty create procrastination and hesitance. Yet the by-product of inaction can be lost opportunities and potentially a sale below market price. Delays can result in the business owner remaining chained to the business and missing out on other rewarding opportunities with family, friends, hobbies, travel and adventure.

There can be temptations to wait for a better offer, a higher price, especially in industries experiencing a lot of acquisition activity. One owner who did this received an all-cash offer that he felt was reasonable based on the acquisition prices paid for other businesses in his industry. He considered delaying, but ultimately decided to act. He said, "If I passed on the offer and the market dried up, I couldn't live with myself. So I took it. Good thing, too. Pretty soon after that the acquisition frenzy leveled off."

The best way to cut through the uncertainties is to learn from others who have gone through the process of selling a business. This isn't a 10-minute conversation at a trade show, but a concerted effort to gain an understanding from multiple sources, including a CPA, an attorney, and business brokers, as well as industry insiders.

"We only got one offer," declared one business owner. She said, "We talked to several of our other industry friends and asked, 'Can you tell us about this? Tell us about your group. Tell me some of the benefits.' The things that were important to them were not necessarily important to us. I felt like we were still on the right track. We would just talk to other people. None of the other groups that we'd asked about felt like the right fit, like the one we were signing with."

"Yeah, it was a little bit of almost too good to be true," said another business owner. "The kind of money that they're throwing around. I never expected that kind of money out of this company. I had trouble believing they're really going to pay me that much money. There was doubt right up until I saw the money in my account. I thought they would say, 'We found something and we're going to back out,' or 'We're going to delay payment on X, Y, and Z' and put us through more mental stress for a couple more weeks or something."

Some owners felt more stress as they neared close, while others felt the stress melt away. "I could just feel, the closer we got, the weight, the 16-ton weights coming off of my shoulders," noted one owner. "And my second-in-command did, too. He could see the weight coming off of my shoulders as well, and he saw that as a good thing."

Selling a business is often a once-in-a-lifetime transaction. As such, it is fraught with uncertainty about the business value, finding buyers, negotiating terms, etc. Business owners facing uncertainty over the sale of the business should seek a seller's representative to assist in the process.

16: Seller's Representative

The importance of an outside representative or agent, such as an investment bank, mergers & acquisitions advisor, business broker, or M&A attorney has been stressed before. There is little question that an agent makes the process smoother, the outcome more certain, and the terms more attractive for sellers. Universally, the sellers who used some kind of agent to assist them believed they fared much better than they would have without one.

For business owners who have no idea how to proceed, a broker or other agent is a necessity. It can spell the difference between making a sale and simply closing the doors. One business owner described what happened when a partnership dissolved and took the business with it. She said, "I started and ran a magazine in New York City for four years. And the unfortunate part of that experience was the magazine was brilliant. We won a lot of awards. But when my business partner and I decided to part ways, it was like the parents got divorced and the child was orphaned and starved in the streets. We didn't have an exit strategy. We didn't know what we didn't know. We had no idea how to go about selling the business, and we really could have. It would have left a really amazing legacy."

Another owner, who used an investment bank, relayed a different story from the magazine publisher. He said, "We wouldn't have known how to market the company. The investment bank we used had the marketing down to a science. They had access to a bunch of databases of prospective buyers and knew exactly how to work them. They were a machine. Our banker waded through dozens of inquiries in response to their marketing, spent a ton of time talking with these guys—a lot of back and forth until we ended up with the finalist. There's no way we would have had time for that without dropping the ball somewhere."

Consider what the business owner is up against. Nearly every business owner is inherently pressed for time, and the process of selling a business boils down to an investment in time. The old saying that *time kills deals* is very true. The longer it takes to finalize the transaction, the greater the chances that the market will cool, the economy will go into recession, interest rates will increase, or any number of other reasons that might cause the buyer to walk away.

One business owner sold his practice just in time. He said, "I sold and it was one month later, they shut everything down. All the other aggregators weren't buying anymore. Practices just shut down. The stock market tanked. So, my timing was perfect. I got the money."

If the economy isn't enough, the longer the process lingers on, the greater the chances of a downturn within the business. Juggling the process without representation means an owner is less involved in the day-to-day operations and more involved in the process of selling the company. Short-term results can suffer, and these short-term downturns can lead a buyer to renegotiate or, worse, walk.

"I never would have gotten it done without a broker," confessed one business owner. "It literally would have just died. Our baby would have starved in the streets. My broker got it done, literally. I had the knowledge and expertise of the business itself, the product, what we're selling. He brought all of the know-how about selling it. He had a list of 7000 people that he would email with the businesses that are for sale. I would have had no idea where to even look to find prospective buyers. That's what he does. He would reach out to some people proactively to bring them to the table."

The business owner went on to draw an analogy between using a professional to sell a business in the same way a professional is used for tax preparation. He said, "If you're running a multimillion-dollar business and you try to do your own taxes without an accountant, there's things that CPAs know that you just don't know. You can't keep up with all the legislation, you can't keep up with the IRS's changes and regulations."

Buyers themselves can also experience setbacks, slow quarters, loss of financing, and changes in strategy. Once the decision is made to sell a business, it's important to keep the foot on the gas pedal. A representative will move the process forward faster, while minimizing (though not eliminating) distractions for the owner.

Business owners often rely on coaches, guides, and professionals. This is just one more. Just like the casual angler hires a fishing guide for a day or two of fishing, it makes sense to hire a guide to help navigate through the unfamiliar, yet critical, process of selling a business. Based on the experience of the business owners interviewed for this book, taking a DIY approach means there is a much higher probability the transaction will not close and a near certainty money will be left on the table.

One business owner was appalled by the notion of a DIY business sale. Commenting on business owners who took that approach, he said, "I think they're crazy. My M&A advisor was worth every penny. I think they're nuts. I'm sure there's some super-smart guys out there, but I've met a ton of owners who sold to private equity and there aren't very many guys, like none, who could do this on their own. I think you'd be leaving money on the table if you tried to handle this on your own."

A private equity buyer who was active in acquiring multiple businesses in a specific industry confessed, "We would rather negotiate with businesses that are represented by a broker or an investment banker. We understand that this means we will pay more, but more importantly it means we will spend less time holding the seller's hand and this frees up our team to focus on other transactions at the same time." While the buyer claimed he did not take advantage of unrepresented buyers, he admitted he did end up paying less when the seller lacked representation.

One business owner discussed the uncertainty of dealing with private equity without representation after being approached about becoming a platform business. She said, "First of all, I was flattered that they would think of me like that. But then, I was scared. Holy crap, I don't know what I'm doing. I don't know anything about the private equity world. I don't want to get taken. If I'm going to do a deal, I want it to be a good deal. And these guys know a lot more about it than I do."

The reason to use some type of seller's representative was summed up by a buyer who said, "It was the biggest decision of my life! If you make some decisions wrong, you can recover. This one, there's no going back if you make the wrong decision."

Business owners who used a representative to assist in the sale of their companies felt they received more money, had more choices, and made fewer unforced errors.

17: M&A Team

It's important to assemble a team to help navigate the process. A lawyer with mergers & acquisitions experience may be the most essential. The typical business lawyer isn't the right person. Lawyers are trained to avoid mistakes, even if it costs the deal. M&A attorneys seek to protect the seller's interests while getting the deal done. M&A is a specialized area. If a law firm lacks this expertise, find another firm with the right specialist to add to your team.

Next to the attorney: A CPA is critical. Not all CPAs and attorneys are equal. Seek out those who have transaction knowledge. Many do not. If your CPA or attorney isn't familiar with business transactions, ask for help finding the right professional. The mere presence of a CPA will reassure buyers. Good financials, with a CPA's blessing, reduce buyer risk. Whenever risk is lowered, the price can rise.

Again, some CPAs and attorneys feel their place is to keep their clients "safe." Accordingly, they provide excessive scrutiny and their default response to any situation is to recommend caution. The intentions might be noble, but this impedes closing a transaction.

In addition, where the business owner and the professional have a long-standing relationship, the professional can be emotionally tied to your business and subconsciously unable to accept that he wants to sell and move into a new chapter in his life.

A business owner discussed how his CPA tried to talk him out of selling. He said, "I used my CPA as guidance when selling my business. He did my taxes for over twenty years and kept me out of trouble more than once. I trusted him. He knew my business as well as my family. He attended my daughter's wedding and we were active in the community together. He was helpful with the sales process, but more than once he felt as if I was selling my business too soon and could get so much more if I were to wait a few years. What he couldn't understand was, for me, it wasn't only about the money. It had to do with the loss of passion and the plan to focus on new projects. The time to sell was then. In the end I had to politely ask him to focus on the taxes that I would owe and not on the purchase price."

Post transaction, sellers are likely to be blessed with significant money. This necessitates two additional specialists, best hired early in the process: a professional financial advisor and an estate attorney.

A business owner described how his financial advisor helped him determine the price he needed. He said, "I used an accountant and a lawyer. I used a lawyer that had worked on 17 practices that sold, and he had done sales with this group eight or nine times. So, he was familiar with their lawyers. It was pretty clean. I had the accountant. I did use a wealth management guy for looking at projections and so forth and so on."

Hiring the right professionals makes sense from the buyer's perspective as well. One private equity buyer said, "When the seller has his real estate attorney who's never done a business sale, it's a nightmare." Buyers want an easier transaction. They do not want to deal with a business owner's buddy from the Rotary Club who does real estate transactions.

The buyer continued, "Getting the deal done is a nightmare without the right people there. So I really try to encourage them to have support. They'll sometimes ask me, 'Do I need an attorney?' I've literally been asked that a couple dozen times, surprisingly. I'll say, 'Yes, you do need an attorney.' They'll say, 'Well, I've got this attorney that I've used.' And I say, 'So, have they done any acquisitions or are they just a business attorney or what? Or is there somebody else in their firm that can do it?' I don't really have the time or interest to teach an attorney what a transaction is about. Some people might try to take advantage of that scenario, I guess.

"I love it when they have a seasoned advisor or a seasoned attorney or CPA or collective group. The least-experienced you think would be easier, but it's almost always harder because then you're having to convince them what market is or what it isn't, or where you're going through the process. I love it when they have that seasoned advisor."

Finally, the buyer warned of the downside to sellers. He cautioned, "You don't want to go through this process without a seasoned advisor because if somebody was unscrupulous, you could potentially be taken advantage of."

"You've got to surround yourself with a team of people that do this professionally," said one business owner. "Most business owners get one shot at selling their business, depending on what age they are. If you're a baby boomer, this is your one shot. If you're 30 years old and you're selling your business, you're going to probably do this a few more times. But still, you've got to have the right team around you to pull it off."

"I learned that you can't have enough lawyers," said another business owner. "I had my personal lawyer, who used to be our corporate lawyer for a while, and then we changed corporate lawyers, so he's now my personal lawyer. I had a corporate lawyer representing the company, even though I owned 100% of the company. There's a lawyer who represented the company and an M&A guy, who is a CPA and an attorney, which is a great combination. So, he took a part in the transaction and put it all together. He said, 'This is what we need to do and when we need to do it. This is what they're going to say. This is what you're going to say back.' He did a great job. He earned every penny he was paid."

Even though some attorneys are also CPAs, it's still advisable to use separate people in each role. "I got connected with a guy who buys and sells businesses," commented a business owner. "I'm talking about very large businesses, not small ones. And he only takes on one account at a time. He won't do any more than one at a time. He is not only a CPA, he's also an attorney. But when he sells a business for you, he doesn't practice for you in either of those capacities. He'll want you to hire your own attorney and your own CPA."

Business owners should assemble an experienced team to help sell their business, including a seller's representative, CPA, M&A attorney, financial advisor, and estate attorney.

18: Betrayals

Virtually anything can happen in the sales process, and the sale can impact a lot of people besides the owners and employees, including suppliers, customers, and competitors. During the sales process, people may act in their narrow self-interest, to the detriment of the business owner, and act in a way that reeks of betrayal. The adage about keeping your head on a swivel applies in the sale of a company. Even if he feels betrayed during the process, the business owner must be able to move past it and stay focused on the end game of completing the transaction.

One seller described how he had an offer for his business but knew a key supplier might be interested, if only for the sales channel. He called the supplier, who sounded excited and said he would get back to him. Instead, the supplier called the seller's financial partners and told them the seller was trying to cheat them, suggesting he was taking money on the side from the buyer. This nearly blew up the deal and certainly lengthened the time to close since the seller had to put the rumors and fears of his partners to rest.

Another seller reported looking at the list of prospective buyers. He said he almost crossed a competitor off the list, but knew they were backed by nearly unlimited capital. They were much smaller, so buying his company made a lot of strategic sense for them. The competitor's principals were either known to him or one degree of separation away. It was a risk, but he let them in.

Upon discovering the company was on the market, the competitor's personnel began spreading rumors in the most harmful way possible that his business was for sale. The seller was forced to spend considerable time reassuring strategic partners that he would stick around and nothing would change. Instead of looking at an acquisition opportunity, the competitor saw it as an opportunity to inflict damage.

"I knew better," the owner remarked. "I knew I should've restricted them from the marketing list but it just made so much sense for them to buy us. Instead, they used the information to crap on us and try to sabotage our key relationships. After that, I'd be damned if I sold to them."

Another owner described how she was betrayed. She said, "We belong to a trade organization and we were at one of their monthly meetings. Another shop owner had seen our business listed for sale. Would you believe he announced it to everybody in the room? I mean, honestly, I could have just kicked him in the cahooties, the little sucker."

A software company was being courted by a larger software business that purportedly wanted to incorporate the owner's company to enhance its offerings. Instead, they used the management meetings to learn everything they could so they could create their own product. The owner said, "People were interested in rolling up companies. My operations guy and I did a presentation to a big software company. We were going to create an alliance with them. They said, 'Well, what if we were to acquire you?' I said, 'Okay, that's viable. You'll become a formidable company. Let's talk about it.' And one of the guys sitting in the room said, 'What if we don't buy you and we just build it ourselves?' I said, 'You certainly can do that.' They said, 'No, we want to let you know that we're not interested in building it ourselves. We'll integrate with your product,' which they never, ever did. They did ultimately create a competitive product that integrates with their software. Those bastards lied through their teeth."

When a business owner feels betrayed, emotions can rage out of control. It's a challenge to rein them in to keep the focus on the process. A successful transaction is the best revenge.

Things will happen in the sales process that seem like betrayals. Some people will break trust if it serves their short-term interests. Business owners should be psychologically prepared for betrayals and ready to move past them to keep the endgame in mind.

19: Management Meetings

If a business owner decides to go to market through an M&A advisor or investment bank, the representative will often set up management meetings with prospective buyers. These are normally half-day meetings where the owners present their business to a prospective buyer, followed by questions and answers.

Management meetings require preparation. The sellers are creating a pitch in the form of a narrative about why their business is awesome and how it possesses a spectacular upside. This is rehearsed over and over with the representative coaching the presenters.

The buyers are similarly presenting themselves as a great home for the business in question. Both sides are selling the other.

After the dog-and-pony show ends, the questioning begins. This is stressful for both sides, but more stressful for the seller. No matter how much rehearsal takes place, buyers can always ask questions the sellers never imagined. For some sellers, this was valuable in itself.

"The management meetings were tough," confessed one business owner. "But it was also incredibly beneficial to have a bunch of really smart people pick apart the company and ask all kinds of insightful questions. I mean, despite everything we spent with an investment bank to get to this point, if it ended right then, it would have been worthwhile because of the improvements we made that were a direct result of things brought out during the management meetings."

Another business owner talked about the importance of selecting the right team to present. She said, "We chose not to tell anyone we were selling. No one in the company knew. My daughter was the only one who knew. And I tried to explain to my sister why she needed to know. She needs to know because when we have to do a management presentation and it's about sales, we have to have someone with some depth who can talk to the future buyer about our sales organization. It can't just be me and my sisters talking. So I brought my daughter in."

If the business is high-performing, highly desired, and in an industry experiencing a lot of acquisition activity, management meetings may take a turn. Instead of the buyers grilling the owner, the buyers *sell* the owner. One business owner recalled, "Each time they pitched to me. They really did try to persuade me. They wanted us. The buyers' whole pitch was about how good they were going to be for my company. I showed them my operation and that was about all

I really had to say about the company, which I was not expecting. I was expecting wining and dining and getting grilled, and having to present everything. That's what the books say to expect. But that's not what happened, I guess in our industry with the feeding frenzy. There are so many buyers, it's a seller's market."

He did note that there were some buyer questions. He said, "They didn't stump me on any questions. I had an answer for every question they came up with. I had a good, solid answer for all of them. They'd ask line-item questions. Why is this an add-back on the EBITDA? I knew my stuff. I explained and they went, 'Okay.' I mean, you go to the industry conferences, you learn all of that stuff."

Not all business owners will experience management meetings. These tend to occur when there's a managed sales process using an investment bank or M&A advisor. Most of the time, the management meetings, even when the sale is being assisted by an M&A advisor, are almost unrecognized for what they are. For example, a prospective buyer flies in and takes the business owner to dinner. It seems like a get-to-know-you dinner, but in fact, it's a form of management meeting.

The owner of an architectural firm described how a buyer flew to his office over the weekend, toured it, then went around to see their work in the local community. This was reciprocated when the owner and his executive vice president flew to the buyer's location. The owner said, "We flew up there. The president picked us up in his BMW 7 series. He's as excited as he can be and gets us into our hotel, and we're meeting that night. We're going to meet for drinks and eat at the biggest steakhouse in the state. I told my EVP, 'No matter what we do, we can't get drunk and make fools of ourselves. Let's try to hold it to two drinks tonight with waters in between.' Because I've seen that happen, and you definitely don't want to blow it by overindulging."

Even when owners plan to sell to an employee or family member, there will still be meetings. The difference is they will be lower-key and less intense.

Given the capability of video calls, such as Microsoft Teams or Zoom, it's becoming more common for management meetings to take place over video conferencing. The intensity of a video meeting is lower, but the business owner must still be prepared to sell the business and be able to answer basic questions. The initial call is essentially a pre-qualifier. If the buyer is interested enough to proceed, the next step is a face-to-face meeting and typically an on-site walkthrough.

There are always management meetings of one form or another as buyers and sellers assess each other. Some are formal, structured meetings. Some are dinners. Business owners should be prepared for all meetings or dinners to be tests for the seller.

20: Intimidation

It can be easy for sellers to feel intimidated by buyers. A business owner described the stereotype: "They arrive in their skinny jeans and puffy vests, flaunting Ivy League and graduate degrees." Faced with the academic pedigrees and financial standing of some buyers, even fairly sophisticated business owners can feel out of sorts.

One business owner recalled sitting in a management meeting where his team was getting grilled by a private equity team. "The thing is," he said, "they were asking brilliant questions about our business that we didn't have answers for. All of us felt just plain dumb... and we have MBAs! Later, we talked with the president of another company who sold to the same PE group. He said the guy asking the most insightful questions was first in his class in Stanford Business School and also first in his class in Stanford Law. He was brilliant, but he'd also never actually run a business."

Another business owner said, "I went into this thinking they were smarter than me. I really did. I thought these guys were smart. My goal when I did this was to learn private equity, because these guys got it going on. I want to understand that side. Well, they're funding. That's all they are. That's what I learned. They are money and not industry experts."

This is key! Even if the buyer is from the same industry, and has operational experience, he won't know the specific business as well as the seller. Most buyers not only lack significant industry and operations experience, chances are good they never built a business or made it work. Whether a business owner holds an MBA or is a high school dropout, he is the expert when it comes to *his* business.

At the risk of offending a PE buyer who fits the stereotype, here are a few intimidating terms business owners might encounter:

- Second Bite of the Apple: This must be the first term learned in PE 101. The "second bite of the apple" involves a seller rolling part of his equity forward into the new entity or fund, which the PE people promise (but never in writing) to sell for three to five times the equity in three to five years. This has worked out well for many business owners, but for others, not so much. Always remember, it's impossible to spend a promise.

- Platform: Usually, PE companies start their groups with a big acquisition, which becomes the "platform" upon which they build. The platform company leaders are often moved into leadership positions of the entire group, but almost always with a CFO who is hand-picked and approved by the main PE fund or partnership.

- Bio-break: For some reason, the money types buying companies don't like to say "bathroom." Instead, they say, "It's time for a bio-break."

- Runway: If there's a lot of opportunity for growth, a buyer will often say, "There's lots of runway."

- Color: When a buyer doesn't understand something, he might say, "Can you add some color to that?"

- Bifurcate: When buyers want to separate something, such as the components of a profit center, they will say, "Let's bifurcate this."

- Unwind: When there's more than two things to separate, the money types will ask to "unwind" it.

- Model: A model, in PE terminology, is usually nothing more than an Excel spreadsheet. "Model" sounds much more sophisticated.

- Ecosystem: Acquired companies often become part of an "ecosystem," which sounds better than a "loose collection of businesses."

- Circle Back: Many people became familiar with the term "circle back" when Biden's press secretary, Jen Psaki, frequently used it to avoid answering a question. Buyers use it when they get stumped and want to leave an issue unresolved so they can move on to something else.

- Helpful: When a buyer wants something from a seller, he will often express it as "helpful." For example, during due diligence, he might say, "A detail of every commission paid by a person from five years ago would be helpful." Business owners might mistake this as a polite request. It's not. It's a demand.

- Lever: If there's an opportunity for one subsidiary to help another, the buyers will say something like, "We can lever this subsidiary to increase sales at that subsidiary."

- Interface: When a couple of buyers meet or talk with each other, they describe it as "interfacing." The buyer will say, "I'll interface with the CFO to see what he thinks."

- Socialize: If a buyer wants to test an idea or business concept, he will say he is going to "socialize" it.

- Straw Man Agenda: A "straw man agenda" is a tentative or rough agenda. The buyer might say, "Let's talk about a straw man agenda for next week's Zoom."

In spite of themselves, business owners will be surprised how quickly they start incorporating the new terms into their own conversations. While buyers might use different language and appear intimidating, it's important to remember that they're just people with different expertise. Business owners should remember that no one knows their businesses like they do.

Buyers, especially private equity, might appear sophisticated and intimidating to business owners. Their expertise is financial. Business owners should take comfort that no one understands their businesses as well as they do.

Jacob and Michel

21: Valuation

It can be hard for a business owner to assess the real market value of his business. Without an idea of the value, the decision to sell now or wait is impossible, except when circumstances compel an immediate exit. Accordingly, many owners procrastinate and wait. This becomes problematic when the delay results in an owner missing the optimal time and circumstances to sell.

One business owner talked about people who waited too long to sell their companies and missed the window of opportunity. "Other people said, 'No, I'm going to hold off and not sell until I can get more money.' It's kind of like owning a piece of property next to a hotel, and the hotel wants to buy your property and you don't want to sell. You wait and wait and wait. In the meantime, the hotel buys another piece on the other side of the building and doesn't want your property anymore. The property only has value because of the guy who's buying it. Nobody else was buying. So there are other people who lost their ass. What's something worth? It's only worth what somebody will pay."

The ways a business is valued will vary dramatically by industry. EBITDA may not be a factor. For example, a pharmacist explained how pharmacies are valued. "It used to be they bought the prescriptions in the inventory, and they still do it that way. That's how they value it. There are pharmacists that open pharmacies just for this reason. They go from zero to 500 prescriptions a day. And you get paid a thousand dollars per prescription, plus your inventory cost. So you can make a couple million dollars real quick if you build it up just by filling prescriptions. Now, that doesn't mean it's profitable.

"Mine was more intangible," he continued, explaining how pharmacies are losing value. "Mine was entirely different. Mine was valued more like a medical or clinical practice where you'd come in, there's old-fashioned pharmacists who would talk to you and look over your medications and your history and see if there's any interactions. It's not like that nowadays. It's more self-serve. So the value of the pharmacy was going down."

A business owner with an established national brand felt there was real value in it. She cut off negotiations with a prospective buyer because he failed to value or recognize the business's brand equity and wanted to price purely on a multiple of EBITDA. She said, "He didn't even value our brand. He said, 'No, we have a formula, X times EBITDA. We don't do any adjusted EBITDA. Take it or leave it.' Okay, great. Thank you. We'll find someone else."

Some business owners have unrealistic expectations of the value of their companies. A buyer said, "Many times I've talked to people about the value of their companies and these guys who have one truck think it's worth a million dollars. You have to be able to get a realistic number that reflects what people are going to pay. And you get that knowledge from a CPA or someone who understands your business and the values of these businesses."

This lack of understanding market value can result in an owner passing on an otherwise great offer. Fortunately, a variety of ways exist for an owner to get a handle on the market value of a company.

Alternatively, some business owners undervalue their companies. One owner was offered more than he expected when a buyer approached him. Skeptical, he assembled a team and tasked them with finding out the real worth of the business. He said, "The first thing we did, as soon as I started talking to these guys, was to involve our CPA and our attorney. I said to our attorney, 'We're having a conversation with crazy people. Find out who they are. Go see if you can find dirt on these guys. Are they legit?' Then I asked our CPA, 'What's this thing really worth? Because we don't think it's worth this. We think this is a very high number. What's this thing really worth?' He came back and said, 'Man, if you can get that, you'd be crazy not to take it.'"

Some owners start with an after-tax amount they need to reach to meet their personal financial goals. This becomes their floor. If they cannot find a buyer willing to meet their minimum, they see little point in continuing the process and elect to continue operating the business. One owner, who jointly owned the business with his father, explained, "I said this is what I need to have to retire and feel comfortable. And unfortunately, that's only half the business. I needed double that in our situation because half was going to my parents and would eventually be divided among my brothers and sisters. The minimum price was somewhat of a red line. We needed to be above this or we didn't even need to talk. I wasn't going to transact under this. One guy lowballed us and we never talked to him again."

Valuations differ by industry. Business owners who talk with people in other industries who sold their businesses can be caught in apples-to-oranges comparisons. A buyer cautioned about this, saying, "The big problem I have is that I typically buy companies at a six or six-and-a-half multiple of EBITDA, maybe seven at the top.

They hear about these 10 multiples and 12 multiples and things like that. So, instead of just going right to where I'm pricing, I lay out their options. I describe it in our industry. Each industry is a little bit different. I've also owned a few tech companies and those are very different situations."

In industries with significant acquisition activity, it's easier to gather information on business value. However, an owner should be aware that his business may not be in the condition or circumstances that match what the market is currently bearing. Moreover, information on recent transactions is often exaggerated or just wrong.

Sellers might overstate the price received in several ways. Some claim a higher multiple of EBITDA because they calculate a different denominator than the market. In other cases, they include earn-outs and other hypothetical earnings. Finally, some sellers' egos result in inflated numbers. Even when they're accurate, they might be one-offs that no one else will attain.

"Just because the market leader of your industry sold his business for a 15X multiple does not mean your business will earn the same," a buyer noted.

There are valuation experts who can assist business owners with a better understanding of what they might expect to be paid. However, not all business valuations can or should be used for determining a sale price. Fair market business valuations or appraisals are designed to produce a value that represents an amount that a willing seller will take and a willing buyer will pay when both understand all relevant facts and neither is acting under any type of compulsion.

This is exactly how the IRS defines fair market value. According to Internal Revenue Service Revenue Ruling 59/60, the term "fair market value" is defined as "the price at which the property would change hands between a willing buyer and a willing seller when the former is not under any compulsion to buy and the latter is not under any compulsion to sell, and both parties have reasonable knowledge of relevant facts."

An example of compulsion would be a private equity investor with a directive to acquire an aggressive number of businesses in a short period. This buyer might willingly pay a premium. Conversely, a seller may be acting under compulsion if the principal faces extreme health issues and must liquidate the business as soon as possible.

One business owner described how he priced his company. He said, "I didn't utilize an investment banker or broker and instead casually mentioned that I was contemplating the sale of my business to an associate over drinks. The associate explained that his business had recently acquired a business not much unlike mine. The conversation started from that point. It gave me a price point I felt confident in because the first acquired business was inferior to mine."

The best measure of value comes from marketing the business to multiple buyers who are competing for the business. Typically, this requires an investment banker, M&A advisor, or business broker. Because they are in the business of maximizing the sale prices of businesses, sellers' representatives have a pretty good idea of the price before the process starts.

While some business owners start with a number they need, others just see what the market will bear. "There was never a number," one seller explained. "We were accepting offers. There was never an asking price. The most dangerous thing you can do is to have an asking price for a business like what you have. You don't want to have an asking price. You want to have at least three buyers who are interested and are making offers. Let them figure out what it's worth."

Of course, when the buyer is a strategic buyer with deep pockets, standard pricing goes out the window. For these buyers, overpaying is less important than securing the business because its strategic value is disproportionate to the price. This happened with one of the owners interviewed. He said, "Our guy said we'd get 23 million dollars. The first couple of offers were in that range. One was 20 or 21. Another was 22. We held out because we thought we had a unique product that would be worth more to the right buyer. Eventually, we hit 30 million dollars."

A buyer said, "If you just want the most amount for your company, go ahead and sign up with an investment banker or broker. Go through a full process. Try to get two or three strategics interested and half a dozen to a dozen private equity groups. But those are typically bigger companies. The strategics aren't going to mess with the typical company."

Sellers should be wary of the sale prices friends and associates report. Misinformation about pricing is rampant. One private equity investor explained misinformation like this: "I was talking to a guy recently and I had approached him about selling his business, and we talked. We had really good discussions, and we were moving along fine. As we get to the LOI, he asked me to give him a ballpark of where I think the value will be. I asked what he was looking for. He said, 'I know such-and-such company sold for 10X.' I told him, 'I actually bought that business and it did not.' I think when people sell, they are a little bit braggadocious. What did you get? I got 10X. You know, it's the big-fish story."

As mentioned earlier, sellers can unintentionally misrepresent their sale price. For example, they might include earn-outs, which are "potential" money and not really part of the sale price. In the sellers' defense, some buyers either imply that the earn-out is part of the sale price or allow the buyer to assume that it is part of the price.

Due to the different ways transactions can be structured, business owners should be wary of accepting at face value the price given to them by peers who sold. Ultimately, the value of a company is determined by the marketplace, understanding that some buyers may pay "above market." To truly assess value, a business owner should be prepared to take the company to market or talk with a valuation expert in his industry.

22: Multiples

A lot of the discussion regarding the sale of a business revolves around the "multiple." This is the multiple of EBITDA. Be careful. The earnings multiple is only one factor in setting a price. While it sounds objective, the actual earnings multiple is a subjective number that can be very hard to pin down.

A seller with a million dollars of EBITDA who negotiates a purchase price of 10 million dollars can say he sold his business for a 10X multiple. However, the buyer may have calculated his purchase price based on anticipated synergies and other factors. Or, assume the buyer makes an internal adjustment to calculated EBITDA and recasts the earnings as 1.2 million dollars. The buyer actually is basing his decision on an 8.3X earnings multiple.

This cuts both ways. Assume that, during due diligence, the EBITDA is determined to be less than one million dollars and comes in at $900,000, yet the buyer honors the 10-million-dollar offering. In this case, the multiple is 11.1!

There are few places where more "multiples talk" occurs than at trade shows, where the conversations often become fishing tales. A private equity buyer said, "No one ever catches a 20-inch fish and tells his buddies it's only 18 inches." This is one of the ways values get exaggerated.

"It's a number people like to focus on," an M&A Advisor noted, "but it doesn't give you the full picture of the value of an acquisition. There's more than meets the eye than someone saying I *received* a 10X multiple. People get too focused on the multiple. I like to tell them, 'Forget the multiple for a minute. What's the sale price you want? What do you need?'"

"It used to be where people had no clue about anything in this process," said a buyer, "no clue what multiples are or anything. Most people, unfortunately, talk about these extreme numbers. As an example, there's a company that has 40 million in EBITDA and it gets a 12 multiple. And so they think, 'My company with two million in EBITDA should get a 12 multiple.' That's not the case. I try to educate them on what reality is. If you had a 40 million or 20 million EBITDA business that was in a market that a strategic wanted, yes, you might pull 12 times. Other than that, that's not going to happen."

An owner who didn't care about multiples said, "We really were looking at a top-line number. I didn't care how they got to it. I have a really good relationship with the buyer today. He gives me a hard time, all the time. He says, 'You know, you guys got the highest multiple ever from us.' Well, I had an expectation and believed we could get it. We did get it. We had two offers that met or exceeded my expectation. My M&A advisor drove these and he handled them masterfully."

Multiples have become a form of scoreboard for many business owners. In the end, the multiple doesn't matter. It's the final number at close that matters.

Many business owners get hung up on multiples of earnings as a price, a number that can easily be skewed. Instead, business owners should determine and focus on the net at closing they want or need.

23: Earn-outs

Without solid advice and representation, sellers are prone to be seduced by the prospect of substantive earn-outs, which are lump sums paid when the seller stays on and certain targets are reached. Earn-outs can be very lucrative, but they must be "earned." They are not a sure thing. As a rule, earn-outs should be treated as ephemeral. Hopefully, the earn-out target will be reached. Maybe it won't. Strive for it, but never count on it.

Some business owners view earn-outs skeptically. "There was no way we were going to accept an earn-out," noted one seller. "It's too easy to manipulate the numbers. All they'd have to do is assign overhead to us and no matter how tight our ship, our numbers would be blown on the expense side. Or they could come in and dictate our marketing spend, killing our revenue."

Earn-outs are put in place to incentivize former business owners to stay involved and motivated. As incentives, they do work. The wife of a husband-and-wife business described how their earn-out motivated them. She said, "We wanted to hit that earn-out goal. The first couple of months started out slow. It was tight that year, but my husband worked really hard. I was helping him. I went back and helped him with marketing without getting paid. We were doing everything so we could keep our EBITDA up so we could earn that earn-out. My husband kept his salary super low, which isn't a good thing, but he did. He kept it down to 80,000 dollars, just so we could do that. I was working and helping with marketing with no pay. He would not take a vacation. He didn't want to leave the office for that year because he wanted it to be tight. He wanted everything to work out and basically worked his butt off. And we hit it, which was awesome."

It should be noted that earn-outs can create an immediate us-versus-them narrative. How can the buyer be trusted to properly account for the financial results of the business post-transaction? If the owner fails to achieve the earn-out for any reason, it becomes all too easy to suspect manipulation on the part of the buyer.

The reality is that buyers *want* to pay the earn-outs to the sellers. This makes sense. If the business performs to the level where that earn-out hurdle is met, it means the acquisition is performing well. If an earn-out is to be part of the transaction, it's up to the business owner to negotiate bulletproof parameters into the stock or asset purchase agreement. This is where an attorney comes into play. A good attorney who understands the pitfalls of earn-outs will be able to structure the terms to increase the odds that the seller will meet the hurdle.

Earn-outs can be a positive component to a transaction if the seller feels he was fairly compensated at close, without considering the earn-out. The earn-out becomes a bonus.

Another positive attribute is that the earn-out gives the business owner a goal with a personal upside if he stays on post-transaction. A short-term earn-out of a year or so provides the business owner with a reason to stay engaged and focused on the prize. This focus can have a positive effect on employee and customer transition.

A business owner with a positive earn-out experience said, "I was guided by my advisor to only take the earn-out if I was happy with the money that I received at close. My brothers (all equal owners) and I were happy with the up-front cash, so we negotiated for a small earn-out. We always looked at the earn-out as icing on the cake. If we got it, then that would be good. The reality is my brothers felt it was unachievable, but I had full intentions on getting it. I stayed on and pushed to meet the buyer's expectations and found that the buyer actually helped us smash the earn-out goal, through cost savings, better training, and marketing support. My only regret is that there was a cap to the earn-out since we blew past the goal. A positive side effect of the earn-out was that it kept me in the game for over a year and, looking back, it greatly helped with the transition for me mentally and for my employees."

Keeping the business owner engaged seems to be one of the best outcomes of an earn-out. "I think the earn-out agreement was very wise," recalled one owner, "because it kept me actively engaged in the business to ensure the success and a successful transfer and the ultimate longer-term success of the business."

"Notes, earn-outs, and rollovers are part of the process in the sale of the business," noted an investment banker. "All three shift additional risk to the seller. Risk can be acceptable if there is a reward to go with it. This is especially the case when a seller rolls over a part of the purchase price and hopes for a second bite of the apple. Over the years, I have had clients who significantly benefited financially from rollovers that paid out. Earn-outs have also been rewarding, especially when there is a clear understanding of how the earn-out will be evaluated, and this is locked in up-front, and carefully documented in the purchase agreement. A seller should NOT bank on a rollover or earn-out to get what he needs from the sale of the business. This should be in addition to the base transaction."

Earn-outs, or performance bonuses, are legitimate means to motivate a newly wealthy business owner who stays on after the sale. Buyers want the owners to achieve the earn-outs because they are performance-based. Business owners should not view earn-outs as a part of the sales price or as something guaranteed.

24: Hold-Backs

No transaction is 100% cash at close, not even an all-cash transaction. Other than limited, small-dollar, small-risk circumstances, there will always be some type of hold-back. Usually, this is placed in an escrow account for a predetermined period of time, such as 12 to 24 months. The buyer gets to tap into the escrow fund if surprise expenses or inaccurate representations and warranties are discovered after the sale.

Hold-backs are usually released from escrow at an agreed-upon date, and when something is taken from the fund, it's usually agreed upon by all parties. It exists as a form of insurance for the buyer.

Buyers will expect sellers to represent and warrant certain claims made about their business. These are typically business characteristics that are impossible for the buyer to understand, even with the most intense due diligence.

A common item to arise in due diligence is lawsuits. The seller will be expected to represent whether or not there are any pending lawsuits or claims. Failure to disclose a pending lawsuit may cause the buyer to retain enough hold-back dollars to cover expenses associated with the lawsuit. Protecting a hold-back requires carefully submitting representations and warranties prior to close. This is one more area where an attorney and investment banker, advisor, or broker will pay for themselves.

If a business owner isn't expecting a hold-back, it might come as a surprise and seem suspicious. It's not. Owners should be prepared to see a hold-back as part of the offer and must make sure the details of the hold-back are clearly understood.

"My deal was all cash, but I was not paid 100% at close," reported a business owner. "The buyer held back one million dollars for 12 months in what was described as a hold-back. I never worried about receiving it. I knew we were a clean business, and the likelihood of a post-close surprise was unlikely. I guess there is always that chance that a buyer might try to find a reason to keep some of this money, but in our case, we were paid 100% immediately after the 12-month mark."

Even with clean businesses, owners worry about receiving the hold-back. They fabricate all kinds of reasons why the buyer might

The Business-Exit Roller Coaster

try to stiff them. It doesn't happen. When money is taken from the hold-back, there is a clear reason and both parties sign off on it.

"A hold-back's been part of every deal I've done," an M&A advisor said. "If you sell a business, you're going to get one. And you're probably going to sweat it, even though you don't need to. Everyone still sweats it and rightly so."

EVERY transaction of any size includes hold-backs placed into an escrow fund to cover surprises missed in due diligence. Barring unusual circumstances, business owners should expect hold-backs and the return of all or most of the escrow at the end of the agreed-upon time period.

25: Seller Notes

Sellers are often asked to accept a note, essentially an IOU, from the buyer. The length of the principal and interest payments will vary. If the note is interest-bearing (and it should be), the seller will be expected to pay taxes on the interest income, even if it's uncertain that the note will ever be paid. If the buyer defaults, the taxes can be adjusted.

Notes are not necessarily bad, but like earn-outs, and depending on the nature of the buyer, sellers shouldn't bank on collecting. Almost all private equity and larger business entities can be counted on to pay the notes. It's when the note is with an individual that there might be some concern. While sellers are paid in the vast majority of cases, seller notes do add an element of risk. When selling a business, be sure that the money at close is sufficient, regardless of the potential from equity rolls, earn-outs, or notes.

"I sold it in tranches, 20%," said a business owner, who explained why she preferred a note. "So, five tranches. There's a contract that, if he defaults, I get the business back. But a lot of owners, when they sell, they don't want the business back. They just want the cash and run with it. With me, I looked at the tax implication of this big lump sum of money in one year to pay taxes on. I'd rather manipulate that over five years."

Another business owner sold to an employee who raised money from relatives and financed the rest through a note when interest rates were low. The owner recalled, "He's got a couple of uncles that are pretty well off. He borrowed some money from them for the down payment. I sold it on a contract. I got a pretty good chunk down. The interest rate he would pay me was prime plus one. Well, you know what interest rates have done since then. His uncles approached him and said, 'We'll take the prime and save you a percent.' They cashed me out."

Notes are more common in a family transaction, where they represent a way for the next generation to pay for the business without a personal guarantee from a lender. This allows the seller to receive a consistent cash flow while maximizing the flexibility of all parties.

A business owner explained how he and his wife purchased a business from his in-laws using a note. He said, "We sat down with the accountant. We had talked about how my wife was going to get the business and how we wanted to structure it. Her parents were ready to retire. And my father-in-law basically told me, 'Keep paying me what I've always made and you get whatever's left over.' I said, 'Why don't you just sell the business? It's going to your daughter anyway. And we'll keep paying you as a consultant, but we'll also pay you off on the note. That way you'll have income for the next 20 years of us paying off the note.'"

A business broker, who dealt with smaller businesses and was very familiar with notes, was cautious about them for business owners who wanted to retire, but otherwise positive. He said, "Notes also are risky. The security of getting one's business back if the buyer fails to pay offers little comfort to the business owner who wants to retire or otherwise move on. Seller notes are common when selling to family members or when selling a very small business. In some cases, the seller may not have an option. One positive [advantage of] a seller note is deferred taxes and, typically, an attractive interest rate. I've been on both the buyer side and seller side of transactions that involved seller notes and, despite seller notes receiving a bad rap, the vast majority of seller notes get paid in full."

A business owner who sold to private equity took a note because the interest rate was attractive. He said, "I took a note for a small percentage of the sale just so we could hit the target price. The kicker was the interest rate they agreed to pay was nearly three times prime, so it wasn't a bad return."

Many employee sales involve a note. For example, one seller said, "I sold my business to an employee and he relied on SBA-backed financing through a bank [SBA lender] for the financing. The buyer wasn't able to come up with the down payment required by the SBA lender. So, in order to get the deal done, I had to carry the down payment in the form of a seller note. The seller note was subordinate to the loan from the SBA lender in all forms, so I have to wait until the buyer pays back the SBA lender before I get anything back on my seller note. Knowing that I will not get paid if the buyer defaults to the SBA lender is stressful, but at the same time, I feel comfortable with what I received on the day of close. If I eventually get paid the rest of the money, it's like a bonus."

Another seller, who accepted a note for part of the purchase, was nonplussed because of his knowledge of, and confidence in, the buyer. He said, "This was a pretty easy decision for me to make. For one, I was selling to a very responsible and known buyer. He was my general manager for the past five years and was incredibly organized and financially responsible. To my knowledge, he was never late on any payment to a distributor. In fact, we were typically a little early.

In addition, this was a friendly transaction and I wanted to streamline the process for him even if it meant still being connected in a small way. I can see how this would be a hurdle for some depending on the buyer but, in my case, it was a no-brainer. Even though our note is subordinate to the SBA loan, I will lose no sleep over this."

Some business owners prefer notes that are paid in installments instead of lump sum. The owner of a franchise said, "When I negotiated my contract, instead of taking all of the money at the time of the close, the franchisee negotiated with me and he held back a million dollars that he would pay me over seven years. And we had negotiated a pretty good interest rate. I actually liked that deal. For me, it worked out well because I went off to do all kinds of different crazy things and I felt like I still had a paycheck."

Notes have their place, especially in sales to family or employees. Yet, even in these cases, the use of SBA-guaranteed loans minimizes the percentage of the sale that must be financed with a note. While business owners might agree to finance part of the sale, they should be clear about the impact of a default and factor in the probability of default. This is far higher for sales to individuals than to corporations or private equity.

Seller notes can be a legitimate means of paying for all or part of a business, depending on the circumstances. They are often used in purchases from family members. Depending upon the relationship and means of the buyer, business owners should consider accepting seller notes in some circumstances.

26: Restrictive Agreements

Although court rulings may change the nature of non-compete agreements in the future, business owners should be prepared to accept them when selling a business. However, the non-compete does not have to be accepted without negotiation. Sellers can negotiate geographic limits. They can expressly and narrowly state the activities considered off-limits. They can seek to reduce the duration of the non-compete.

Regardless of the time and geographic limitations, the business owner must be prepared to sign a non-compete agreement. Non-competes exist for a reason. Buyers do not want to purchase a business only to see the seller open a similar one soon after the transaction closes. Even with a non-compete, some owners, especially younger ones, start counting the days until they can get back in the game.

"Oh, trust me," said one seller, "everybody on my management team has already planned their retribution if [the buyers] still own the company. It's just not top-of-mind. By then, I may have a different mindset, but I am going to talk to a friend who sold. He is getting stuff figured out. He's a little bit ahead of me."

Five years for a non-compete is often the starting point for buyers, though the length can be negotiated. An M&A advisor said, "On the deals I do, when you're selling to private equity, you're not going to be able to work in your three counties for five years. Everybody's okay with that."

"Will I dip my toes back in? You know, I could at some point in time," said another business owner. "I negotiated a really short non-compete. They wanted five years. I got them down to two."

He went on to explain that his motivations would be different for the next company. He said, "Now it's about legacy. So, it's a little different. I've accomplished at least what I need to do for my family. Now it's what can I accomplish for me as a professional."

There are situations where "carve-outs" can be considered when negotiating a non-compete, and this should be kept in mind. An example may be a veterinarian who sells his small-animal practice. If the selling veterinarian wants to continue to practice on large animals, this could potentially be addressed in the non-compete agreement.

Non-competes can have their quirks. "My non-compete is very, very stringent in my home state," commented one business owner.

"But the state next door, which is literally 30 minutes from me, I have zero non-compete."

Another business owner said, "They also wanted us to sign a three-year employment agreement, to stay on for three years. We were both okay with that. It was a non-compete. We couldn't leave the firm for three years. And if we did, we couldn't do business within 100 miles of the offices and whatever. That was no problem. We wanted to see the office succeed."

The ins and outs of the legal nuances of a non-compete agreement should be left to an attorney. Also, enforceability can vary by state, which a local attorney can clarify.

In addition to the non-compete are non-solicitation agreements in which the business owner agrees not to solicit customers or recruit employees for a period of time. Finally, the owner might be asked to keep the terms of the sale confidential and to not disparage the buyer.

"I signed a non-compete," said one owner. "It was a no-brainer and, going in, I expected to have to sign one. My non-compete was for five years. What was more surprising is the agreement not to hire my employees. The buyer seemed to be more concerned about this than the non-compete."

What happens if a business owner refuses to sign a non-compete? It can kill the transaction. A business owner discussed how his partner had second thoughts over a non-compete. He said, "My business partner started having cold feet on the non-compete part of the sale agreement. She thought it was too restrictive and had a bad previous experience where she sold a business. The buyer said that she violated the non-compete and kept the escrow. She wouldn't sign on our transaction and the lawyers wouldn't change it. It was an impasse that affected my relationship with her. It was tough. The buyer said they couldn't spend any more time on this. Either we're doing this or not. They had to move to the next deal."

The business owner's partner wouldn't budge. He said, "She thought it was a trap. She thought that it's so restrictive she was going to go do something and they're going to come after her. She really feared that. Ultimately, we compromised where she got 100% at close and I absorbed her portion of the hold-back."

Every business owner is confronted with the requirement of a non-compete agreement. Sellers are being fairly compensated, so this should be expected. In addition, a non-solicitation agreement will also likely be requested, if not included in the language of the non-compete. Non-disparagement agreements might also be required. Business owners should be prepared for them, though they can negotiate the duration, geography, and breadth of the agreements.

> *It is normal and expected for business owners to sign non-compete, non-solicitation, and non-disparagement agreements. After all, the owner is receiving significant money in compensation. Business owners should expect them and expect to sign them.*

Jacob and Michel

27: Building Access

Most buyers want access to a seller's building. Simply put, they want eyes on what they are purchasing. If a walk-through shows that the seller runs a tight ship, buyer risk is reduced. If, on the other hand, the operation looks chaotic, risk increases. As simple as it may sound, the way a building presents itself goes a long way.

The office visit can be a significant emotional hurdle for many business owners. The most common concern is that a hyper-alert employee will sense something's up. It's not an unwarranted fear. Employees guess correctly all the time when an owner is selling the business, and a group of strangers receiving the full tour is certainly a clue.

The good news is that buyers are flexible and understand this concern. Business owners use a variety of approaches to allow buyers to see their facilities without letting employees know. Some wait until the evening or a weekend for a walk-through. Others portray the buyers as insurance representatives, customers, industry associates, or auditors.

If possible, the after-hours approach is cleanest. Portraying a buyer as a visitor starts the relationship between the employees and the buyer with a lie. Moreover, there's a good chance that at least one of the employees has been through that lie before and will see right through it.

Unless the buyer insists upon seeing the business in operation, plan to conduct the visit after hours. One owner commented, "We were reluctant to bring the buyer into the building because we are a small office and it would have been difficult to do the walk-through without it raising red flags with employees. Our buyer understood and we ultimately scheduled a visit for after hours. I was nervous about what to expect from the walk-through, but it was really not that big of a deal and it lasted less than an hour."

Another commented, "I said, look, we can't bring you in and parade you around our offices during the week. We just can't do that. You need to come up on a Friday, and we'll take you to the offices on Saturday and/or Sunday. We'll drive you all around and show you some of the projects that we've worked on."

While the visit to the office can be a stressful step in the sale process, it doesn't have to be. Buyers want to see what they're buying and if the existing building can sustain the business initially and through the planned immediate growth. "The office or facility visit should not be feared," said an M&A advisor. "It's a necessary step and the more open and forthcoming the seller is about it, the better. Besides, the on-site visit is a great time for the seller to get to know the buyer better. It usually happens after the buyer treats the seller to a nice dinner. I have had clients who refused any form of on-site visit until the transaction was complete and this refusal added to the buyers' transaction skepticism."

> **Business owners must be prepared to allow buyers building access, though not necessarily during working hours. The business owner should understand that the buyer needs access and is making an intangible assessment of the company based on the condition of the facilities.**

Jacob and Michel

28: Negotiations

Negotiations of the terms and conditions of the Letter of Intent involve agreeing on the core components of the business transaction. The LOI is not intended to contain 100% of the transaction details; certain details are hashed out later when the stock or asset-purchase agreement is finalized. Details such as the seller's compensation post-transaction if he stays on, building lease terms, and so on are commonly left out of an LOI. These are finalized as the transaction moves to close and give the buyer a better understanding for the business going forward. That being said, signing the LOI and understanding the terms and conditions outlined in it represent a pivotal point of a business transaction.

Several sellers entered into LOIs with the false belief that the terms and conditions will change significantly. Although a buyer can and will re-negotiate an LOI if due diligence reveals unfavorable findings within the target business, renegotiations and retrading should not be expected. As a rule, negotiations should proceed as if the price and terms and conditions agreed in the LOI are final.

Until the LOI is signed, everything is negotiable. After signing, attempts by the seller to negotiate can squelch a deal. Thus, business owners should consider items that are personally important to them prior to signing the LOI. This could include a favorite truck that the seller would like to retain, a laptop, a phone, office furniture, artwork, and so on. The time to discuss these is before the LOI is finalized. One business owner specifically requested that he keep all office taxidermy, including a full-body mounted black bear.

"We were ready to sign to LOI as we liked the dollars offered and the terms," said a business owner. "Prior to signing, our advisor suggested that we think long and hard about all the personal items within the business that we might want to retain. We carved out my truck and laptop and some sentimental tools that were my father's when he started the business. This turned out to be good advice. We didn't have to ask for them later."

Another business owner made sure his personal health insurance was part of the deal. He said, "Part of my buy-sell agreement was that my health insurance is paid in the same policy I have now until I'm 65. So I'm not going to have to worry about that."

The lead-up negotiations to the letter of intent aren't the most trying phase of a business transaction simply because, at that point, neither the seller nor the buyer has a significant amount of time and emotions invested in the transaction. The mood of the pre-LOI period is like casual dating. Afterward, it's an engagement. Sellers interviewed for this book expressed elation when the LOI was signed. Most agreed that the heavy lifting started after the LOI was signed.

"The best day of the entire transaction was the day I signed the LOI," said one business owner. "This is when things became real. I could see the money in my head and imagine what I could do with it. I had yet to go through the trials of due diligence or working for the new owners."

Another owner described his negotiation. He said, "It wasn't really a whole lot of back and forth. I can't remember specifically how we arrived at the number, but it ended up being right at five million dollars. And that was in multiple layers, stock, cash, a payout, and assets. It was well thought out. When we got to that number, I said, 'Look, guys, I think I'm being very generous here, and I think I'm leaving a lot on the table, so I think an extra 150,000 dollars up-front isn't going to hurt you too bad.' They just looked at each other and said, 'No problem.' That was too easy. Maybe I didn't do enough negotiating at the table."

Unfortunately, not all buyers negotiate in good faith. One business owner described his experience. He said, "I excused myself out of my sister's deathbed. Literally, she was on her deathbed. I went in the hallway and I'm talking to somebody from the buyer, and they're yanking my chain as far as the sell price, which I know is a part of the process."

Frankly, it's not part of the process, and this is another case where a business owner would have been well-served by a seller's representative. He continued. "I said to them, 'You know what? This negotiation is over. My sister's in the next room. She's got days to live, if not hours. We're done. Piss on it. I'm not calling you back.' You see, not only was I selling my business and going into another chapter of my life, but I had my only sibling on her deathbed. We knew it was close. And somebody's trying to yank my chain? I said, 'If you don't want my business don't buy it. Goodbye.'"

The buyer was trying to renegotiate their LOI. The business owner said, "I got that feeling that was their M.O. But I heard from other people who ultimately did sell their businesses that they had the same experience. I'm not here to blast them. Their purpose in life is to buy cheap and ours is to sell expensive."

In the end, the business owner went back to the buyer and was able to flip the script. He demanded a higher price and got it.

Another example of bad-faith negotiations occurred with a seller who was using an investment bank. While visiting the operations of a suitor, the buyer presented a low-ball offer directly to the business owner without including the investment banker. "I was pissed," said the owner. "My partner was pissed. The investment banker was even more pissed. They knew they screwed up when we just got up, left, and called an Uber for the airport. They compounded it over the weekend when they upped the offer by four million dollars and called me direct, again cutting out the investment banker. The four million dollars was contingent on me and my partner staying with them for five years. I said it would have to be in escrow and payable on demand if we were terminated for any reason. He said that's not going to fly. I said, 'So you can terminate us after four years and eleven months and save four million dollars, plus interest? You are freaking insane.' If they did this before the transaction, imagine what they would be like post-transaction. No way were we selling to them."

Before signing the LOI, everything is negotiable. While non-binding, the LOI essentially locks in price, terms, and conditions. Signing the LOI is a high point in the sales process because it's all possibilities and no pain. Business owners should make sure all of their requirements are included in the LOI before signing.

29: Equity Rolls

Private equity buyers will often offer sellers a "second bite of the apple." The goal is to entice the seller to roll equity forward into a platform company, a new enterprise that's created alongside the execution of the transaction, or some other acquiring business. If the seller rolls money forward, that's money that the buyer won't need to pull from his existing war chest or finance with debt.

The roll has a second, maybe more important function for the buyer. It ensures there continues to be a financial stake on the part of the seller. If the buyer plans on keeping the seller around to operate the business, the roll becomes motivation to perform.

Business owners should be aware that the money rolled forward is out of their control. Even if they walked away from the business completely, they must wait until the new entity flips ownership or goes public to get their money out. If things go sideways, they may not get their money out at all.

On the whole, business owners are more likely than not to be control freaks. It's a trait that comes with the territory. Having a significant sum of money completely out of their control grates on them. Even if there's no reason to worry, they struggle with it.

A business owner who quit two years after he sold, and was full of angst watching his successor make what he considered to be a series of bad moves, was asked why he cared. "Well," he said, "because I'm heavily invested in it. Contractually, I can't do anything about the money I rolled. I think that's the biggest thing that's upsetting me the most right now. My wife and I have spoken. We've thought about just trying to give back our stock [rollover] and say, 'You can have it. Let me out of my non-compete, because I'll build a company in a year's time that makes that money back up.'"

The second bite of the apple is seductive. Private equity buyers often imply, but never promise, a 3X to 5X cash-on-cash return in two to three years, if not sooner. The truth is that a seller may get that kind of return or may not. It may be in two to three years or may take much longer. For this reason, it's wise for sellers to be satisfied with the up-front money, regardless of the roll. They should consider equity rolls speculative. If it works out (and it usually does), it can deliver a spectacular payoff. If it doesn't, the owner should be content with the money received at close.

When deciding how much to roll, the happiest business owners are those who took an analytic approach. They figured the money desired at close plus a generous fudge factor as a baseline. Any equity roll was limited to the funds above the baseline. An owner described this approach. "My wife and I figured out what it would take for us to survive. We knew how much money we needed if we wanted to live off the investment return. We put 50% on top of it and this was the minimum we needed at close. They offered us more than our number. So, the reinvestment was fun money. We know these windows [to sell the stock purchased from the equity roll] open and close. We know we may be able to buy our company back for pennies on the dollar. We know all these things are possible. Or, we could have had three turns and make another 40 million dollars. When we invested 30% of the business sale price forward, it was fun money at that point."

Many business owners feel a sense of obligation to roll money forward. If the buyer believed in them, they feel they should believe in the buyer. Few, if any, buyers base their offers on a belief in the owners. They base it on their projections of the business's future profit potential or because the business fits a strategic need. Nevertheless, it's common for owners to feel the pull of obligation. They should be aware that this is a purely emotional response.

"I think that I figured that if they believed in me this much, I should believe in them this much," said a business owner.

"I rolled the maximum forward that they would let me," noted another owner. "I felt like they were showing faith in me by giving me all of this money for my company and this was how I could show faith in them. Plus, if I'm honest with myself, I got a little greedy and bought into the story they were telling me about flipping the business."

As much as business owners might hesitate to admit it, greed definitely factors into equity roll decisions. An owner described how it factors. "There's the FOMO [fear of missing out]. I mean, 110%. Keep in mind, a lot of my friends sold during the height of the acquisition frenzy. They got 9X or 10X when they sold. If they rerolled five million of their 20 million dollars, at a 3X return, their five million dollars is worth 15 million dollars. I thought, 'Oh my God, you can triple your money. I should put more into this.' It felt emotionally like it was a fairly sure thing, like an 80% to 90% guarantee that it was coming back triple. That's what I felt like in my mind. Looking back, it sounds so stupid. At the time, it felt way too real."

While equity rolls have tremendous upsides, not every rollover works out. A business owner who failed to realize anything from the money he rolled forward said, "I've always read that if somebody loses their legs, they go back to their normal happiness level within 30 days. It probably took me 45 days from the day that I realized the 18-plus million dollars I'd reinvested went to zero and was not going to come back. There was the full grieving scale. But at the same time, I'm very fortunate. I don't want it to come off as a sob story or a woe-is-me. Other sellers I know have done very well with their reroll. So, there's a lot of people that have won there."

He described how he felt when he realized the equity roll was lost. "When it became evident that the rollover was in jeopardy, it was like there was a death in the family. I'm sure many would say, 'Oh, it's just money.' That's what my wife said. She said, 'We didn't need it.' I got mad at her. I said, 'What do you mean, we don't need it? It's ours. It's not somebody else's. We worked hard for this, and my team worked hard for this.' And once again, my team reinvested one to two, three million dollars. When my team reinvested two to three million dollars of their money, I felt like I had a fiducial responsibility to my team. They were kicking ass. I was kicking ass. The majority of the companies were kicking ass. It was the equity group that was mucking it up and they wouldn't take responsibility. They wanted to blame everybody but themselves."

Overall, more business owners had success with rolling equity forward than failures, though the failures tend to be more vocal. It should also be noted that many of the business owners interviewed had sold so recently that the jury was still out. Regardless, when considering how much to roll forward, it's easy to get seduced by big numbers and make an emotional, rather than a rational, decision.

One business owner who felt like he got a good return noted, "While my decision to roll equity forward was more emotional than rational, it worked out in the long run. It took six years, but the compound annual growth rate was 18%."

Another business owner noted that he saw several companies do extremely well with second bites. "But," he added, "I've seen the other, ugly side of it. My buddy had a 42-year-old business that was gutted in seven weeks. They never moved in. They're still paying rent for two years on an empty office."

Sellers need to check with their attorneys and accountants to see if the money they roll forward is recorded as taxable income or is a tax-deferred rollover. If taxable, the taxes will need to be paid from the cash received at close, lowering the available cash, after taxes. If it's a tax-deferred rollover, the seller won't pay taxes until the receipt of the second-bite money.

Taxes can be a major consideration when looking at the percentage rolled forward. It's common for buyers to ask sellers to roll 20% to 40%.

Buyers will often ask business owners to roll equity forward for a "second bite of the apple" when the new enterprise is sold or taken public. While this can be incredibly lucrative, it should never be assumed to be a sure thing. Owners should be satisfied with the cash received at close and treat the equity roll as separate.

30: Selecting a Buyer

Lots of factors go into the selection of a buyer. Obviously, the money has to be right, but once that's addressed, cultural consistency is a major consideration. Sellers will sacrifice some of their return for a buyer who appears to respect what's been built and indicates a desire to carry it forward.

One owner commented on the importance of a cultural fit. He said, "We rejected the best strategic fit because the PE guys backing them were jerks. Ultimately, we picked the company whose culture most closely matched ours."

Strategic fit does matter to some owners. One owner who was attracted to the strategic-growth potential of the selected buyer said, "The buyer had 16,000 customers who were all potential candidates for our products. The same was true in reverse. And there were other subsidiaries who aligned with our products. It looked like a cross-marketing dream where it wouldn't take much effort for us to grow exponentially."

Beyond strategic fit and culture is the opportunity for personal growth, especially for younger owners. This was the deciding factor for a 40-year-old owner who said, "My partner and I looked at the money truck backing up, but we also looked at the educational opportunities. We thought, who's going to give us an education like these guys? They had some cutting-edge, unique financing practices we wanted to learn about. As things get more expensive, affordability is going to be more important. Leasing is probably going to be a bigger player, and we wanted to figure out how all this stuff works. In our case, it wasn't just the money, but the education."

Buyer sensitivity to the tax implications of a sale can also be significant. One business owner discussed how taxes affected his decision. "I sold to a publicly traded company. I talked to private equity, but the main reason I went with the public company was they would buy my stock, not my assets. The only way I would sell was a stock deal. I was a C corporation and I owned 100% of the stock. If I sold the assets, the gains were taxable at regular income rates, but if I sold the stock, then it's a long-term capital gain."

While every seller wants to maximize the sale price, many might be surprised by how often a seller rejects the highest offer. Apparently, there's a point in many sellers' minds where a certain amount of money is sufficient. Above this threshold, other factors can take priority.

"We actually had multiple offers in the 50-million-dollar range," said a business owner. "The one we took wasn't the highest offer. We actually took the second-highest offer because of the way they promised to treat our employees and the way they talked about what our work life would look like."

Another business owner said, "Cultural fit was really important for me. We had a super, super-strong culture. I actually went and visited one of the finalists. They didn't know that I was coming to see them because they were a tiny customer of ours. I remember going in there and the owner was so full of himself. I pretended like I didn't know that they were looking at us, and he pretended like I didn't know that they were looking at us. I'm walking around the building and thinking, *What an idiot.* They were very old school. I took him off the list because I thought, *It's not going to be a cultural fit.*"

Hollywood portrays businesspeople as greedy and purely money-driven. In fact, most businesses aren't started with the idea of making the most money possible. Michael Gerber, author of *The E-Myth,* says that most businesses are started because an employee gets mad and, in Gerber's words, fires the boss and goes to work for a lunatic, who is himself. The primary reason most people start a business is not to make more money, but to gain more control and independence. Thus, it shouldn't be surprising when, at the end of the day, money is not the driving factor behind the selection of a buyer.

One owner described how money was a minor factor when he acquired a competitor. "The couple running the company were just flat-out tired. Their kids saw what the business did to their parents and, while they worked in the company, they wanted no part in running it. A few companies sniffed at them, but ultimately didn't want the business, so I approached them. I knew through the grapevine that they were considering just closing the doors, but were worried about their customers and their employees. I told them that I'd take care of their customers the way they took care of them. I'd keep all of their employees, including their kids, and they could keep their inventory and physical assets and sell it for whatever. I didn't make them a great offer financially, but combined with their faith in how I would take care of everyone, it was enough for them to feel good about walking away."

A pharmacist explained why he refused to sell to a chain. "Within the retail side, what we call community pharmacies, there's chain and independent. The chains are the big ones that take over. They destroy a practice. All they're focused on is efficiencies and distribution. The independent pharmacy, the mom-and-pop store, is more focused on customer service, in my case, more patient care. I never wanted to sell to one of the big chains because I always felt like my practice had patients where in a chain, you don't have patients. You don't even have customers. You have just numbers, because it's all distribution-based. So that's why I sold to the local independents."

Another business owner was concerned about the business practices of the buyer for his company. He said, "I did feel a responsibility to my employees and to my customers. Our town has 250,000 people and my name's on the business. I'm going to interact with these people post-retirement in our community in many ways. The thing that was scary to me was selling to somebody I didn't know or selling to private equity and then having them make decisions that I would strongly disagree with. And I knew I would have no control over it. So a good fit was probably the most important thing to me."

An M&A advisor doesn't buy into owners' proclamations about seeking the best fit. He said, "This is so subjective, and in reality, my personal experience is that sellers say they want the best fit, but 99% go with the money. Lately, it has been all about money. A few years prior to that it was, *Can we find a buyer?*"

The reality of most business transactions is that there isn't enough time or information to guarantee the seller is making the right choice about the intangibles. Only the financial points spelled out in the LOI are objective. A seller may use a broker or investment banker to drive the sale of the business into an auction, resulting in a superior purchase price and transaction structure, but the seller still may not have enough information to be able to choose the best buyer in terms of non-financial concerns.

"A wise seller defines what is truly important to him and makes that a priority when 'interviewing' potential buyers," said an investment banker. "Of course, sellers must understand they are selling their businesses. Once the transaction is closed, they no longer call the shots. The buyer can (and will) do whatever it takes to make the investment work out. Some of the decisions made by the new owner may not be tolerable to the seller, but it's not the seller's company anymore. He sold it."

An owner who didn't fully explore the market, and who believed that one private equity group is pretty much like another, learned after the fact that fit and culture vary among private equity buyers. He said, "When I start to learn about other groups and some of the things that they do and that makes them unique, I think, 'Oh, man, I kind of wish I would have known more about you before we sold our company. You sound like a really cool group to be part of.' I wish I would have explored more groups instead of just gone with the first one."

To reassure business owners about their companies, buyers, especially private equity buyers, will often provide a list of people who owned companies the buyer had already purchased. There's a danger of putting too much stock in the information provided by the former owners who were acquired, though. A business owner explained, "You can call and talk to their other companies and they'll fill you full of crap because it's going to make their stock go up." He believes he would get better information from friends who sold. He said, "I would probably go with somebody where my friends are already on the platform and could tell me what the real deal was."

The business owner assumed, of course, that his friends wouldn't also talk up the company, whether the decision was a good one or not. Some people may not accept that they made a mistake and speak well of the business in an attempt to internally rationalize their decisions.

In the most unusual situation encountered in the research for this book, one owner identified a buyer, negotiated a deal, then gave each person on his leadership team the right to kill the deal. He described how he presented this to his leadership team. "We're at the dinner and I said, 'Tomorrow morning we're going to the club and we're going to sit down with the owners. They've brought their ownership team in and they want to meet you and then we're going to talk about this in case we don't want to do it.' I said, 'I'm giving each one of you a blackball. And if you don't like this deal, you don't have to say why. All you got to do is drop the blackball and we won't do this, for real. If you're not 100% in, I'm not going to do this because it's about you. It's about the future of the company. And if you don't see the vision, then I'm not going to do it because it's not about me.'"

No one on his team objected. This was also the smoothest of all of the acquisitions examined. He added, "I asked them later why they were okay with the acquisition. My office manager said, 'We would follow you through a fire. You've never led us wrong. You've never hung us out to dry. You've always done what you said you were going to do. And we believe that you've got the vision that some of us don't have because we're doing the work.' Man, that kind of choked me up. I was really touched by that. And another guy said the same thing. And another said the same thing."

Selecting a buyer really comes down to money and fit. If the money's insufficient, fit takes a back seat. Once the money works, fit becomes a consideration. Business owners should select buyers based on money first, fit second.

Jacob and Michel

31: Reading in Team Members

Business owners almost universally dread telling their teams they are selling. Eventually, they must, though some wait until the day after the transaction is complete and share the burden of communication with the new owners. By contrast, some are so completely up-front and open that they give key people veto rights over the sale, as discussed earlier. This is one area where there is no consistency.

Many business owners fear the possibility that their employees will discover the business is being sold. One noted, "I was just trying to hide everything from my employees. You don't know it's going to close until it closes, until you're paid. The last thing you want to do is have your employees find out. What if I go through this and they all find out and then the deal doesn't go through and then I come to work the next day and then, *boom,* everybody's going to start leaving? That was the battle that I faced for quite a bit."

Fear that employees will quit if they discover the business is for sale is common among business owners, if not quite rational. "I really didn't want our employees to know that I was going down these paths because I was afraid of losing some people," said a business owner.

Adding stress for owners who fear losing people is the fact that some employees guess or presume the business is for sale. Their ability to predict a sale is like an economist's ability to predict a recession. The old joke about economists is that they've successfully predicted ten of the last two economic downturns. Similarly, employees often erroneously predict a sale is in the works when none is pending. Invite an unknown guest into a closed-door meeting and the rumors start. An owner attends to a private, personal matter that takes him out of the office with no explanation and the rumors start. Thus, it shouldn't be a surprise if they eventually guess correctly. Even a broken clock is right twice a day.

A business owner who knew he would eventually sell began preparing his team years in advance. He said, "I thought they may be afraid of the future. So, whether this is right or wrong, about five years ago, intentionally, I would call a meeting and say, 'You guys have probably heard the rumors that we're selling the company, and someday we will, but we're not right now. And when the time comes, I'll let you know.' I just wanted it planted in people's heads so when the time really came, it wouldn't concern the employees as much as it might if it came out of the blue. So that's kind of how I set the stage."

Another owner explained that he created a story to explain the presence of people reviewing his financials and other information. "You need to have a cover story. The cover story we had was *It's for insurance*. And we did get a few eyes this way and eyes that way, but, boy, this insurance company is really thorough. He's in the back room going through all the books and asking for this and asking for that and computer printouts and everything, all for insurance."

Nature abhors a vacuum. So do people. One business owner took pains to kill rumors before they got started. "I always took great care of how the employees learned of things. I always feel if you don't tell your employees what's going on, they just make it up in their head."

Yet employees are more tuned into management's behavior than most owners suspect. When the sale of one business was announced, the owner confessed, "No matter how hard you try not to let it out that you're selling, they figure it out. The buyer did one walkthrough. And that was at the lunch when we met the buyer, a month earlier. That was the only time he had been in the building. Yet the employees already had an inkling of what was going on."

There are also times when word just gets out. A business owner said, "It leaked. When the buyer sent guys out to do the due diligence and started showing up at the different branches, they didn't follow the instructions. One guy just came right out and told my salespeople that I was selling and they were there to have a look at stuff. What a dummy! But I was prepared. I already had an announcement written. When it hit the fan I immediately sent it out, much to the chagrin of the buyer. I told the buyer, 'Look, your guy leaked it out. I had to do something. I have to tell my employees what's going on.'"

While the employees may not discover the business is for sale before a business owner is ready to read in the team, he should be prepared for them to find out. If word does get out, owners must act fast in their communications if only because having the team on board is beneficial to the sale of the company.

When his people started to find out the company was on the market, a business owner immediately called a companywide meeting and addressed their concerns. "A couple of the more connected people found out the business was on the market. I called an all-company meeting the next day and said we were exploring ways to raise capital. I said we needed more capital to grow at the rate we wanted and needed to grow, that I wasn't leaving, and didn't expect anyone else to leave. I said if we didn't find the right people we wouldn't move forward with their investment. That was true. Once I reassured everyone that they would still have their jobs, concern went away."

Another business owner described how an employee found out the company was on the market before there was an announcement. He quit and told other employees they should quit, too. The owner said, "I went around and tried to soften it all up. And, honestly, the rest of the team didn't give a flying flip that the business was selling. They were just grateful that the new guy was going to keep them."

Employees are tuned into WII-FM (What's In It For Me). They want to know how the sale of a business will impact them personally. Most are content if it's neutral or positive. It appears surprisingly easy to convince people that the grass will be greener with new owners who want to invest.

Employees tend to be mercenary. While business owners feel a sense of loyalty from their employees is their due, these same loyal employees recognize who is signing their paychecks and dish out their loyalty accordingly. Thus, loyalty reallocates with pay.

If the employees don't discover the business is for sale before the owner announces it, the day will come when he needs to let the team know. Small businesses have more options for reading in the team. One owner believed it was better to tell people one-on-one and avoid the potential for one employee to set a negative tone in a group situation. He said, "The vice president came in and sat down there with an employment package for each person. He explained that they decided to acquire this company. Here is the opportunity for you as an individual. So each person came in privately, sat with him privately, and got to hear what the sales pitch was. Because we did keep it confidential, it was allowed for the employees to be sold individually. It certainly was a benefit to them. Everyone could see it. So, that one little step where someone with that soft touch was able to make that sale. We didn't do it in a group setting, where you get one guy who can go negative in front of everyone. It's easier one-on-one. You can handle conflict with that one person or any objection that one person might have."

Some business owners stress the importance of informing their teams themselves. One explained, "We didn't care about anything other than people finding out about the sale from someone besides us. I'm sure everyone thinks this, but we really felt, and still feel today that our people trust us. We do everything we can to take care of them and be good people. Having our people find out some other way was just terrifying to us."

Even when the owner tells people directly, there can be hard feelings about being left out of the loop. An owner described this, saying, "We set up a meeting with our leadership team, just the leadership team, and told them. I do think there was a period of a couple months when we lost trust of our leadership team, which was unforeseen. We had broken a trust. We made a huge decision and didn't loop them in in any way. They didn't have any say in it. There's an emotional tie. You're going to break some trust. You're going to let some people down. There's going to be people who feel they were duped. They said, 'I thought I knew you. I never thought you would sell the business.'"

Surprisingly, there are business owners who don't even make an announcement. "I sold 80% of my business and retained 20% in an equity rollover," said one owner. "Technically, I was still the owner and I was not going anywhere. I agreed to stay and run the business. I made the decision not to say anything to anyone other than my key managers. The investors were not going to have a day-to-day role in operations. They actually preferred that there was no big announcement."

The big announcement, however, seems to be the norm. "We had a really nice breakfast. We get up to tell them the good news. I really believed that this was a better thing for them with more opportunity. I really just had to paint the picture for them, all of the benefits. And my whole goal going into that was not to lose any employees. I love my team. I had a solid team. We wanted to go through the sale and not have anyone leave and everyone stayed on. We didn't lose one employee."

One business owner closed on the sale of his business a month after moving into new offices. At the celebration for the new building, he broke the news. He said, "We had a company-wide meeting to kind of celebrate this new office. We had the new owners fly in and wait at a Starbucks down the street. I read my script of three or four pages of history, how we had grown, and different offices that we'd been in, the projects and everything. A lot of people were thinking, *Oh my gosh, he's getting out, he's selling, he's whatever.* Then I said we are going to now be a part of a large out-of-state engineering firm. And with that, the new owners came down the hall. Some people turned white as a ghost. We wanted to assure them they weren't coming in and cherry picking. They were bringing 100% of our people in. They were bringing 100% of the pay, 100% of the seniority. They came up with the same amount of vacation. Nobody was going to get dipped in any way. It had to come in as seamless as possible. And once the employees found out that was the case, there was a big sigh of relief across the room."

Some business owners seed the audience with supportive people by reading them in first and asking for their help. For example, a business owner told two of his key people the night before he told his team. He stressed that he needed them at the meeting the next morning. He told them, "I need you to be the biggest cheerleaders to the team."

When the announcement is made, it's important to sell the change. Telling the team and customers, if appropriate, is a marketing exercise. One business owner said, "I'm a storyteller, so I can tell you the stories around it. Think how you handle communication with your employees and your clients. You should think about that more than the day before or the day of the transaction. I do marketing strategy. That's what I do for a living. So I always put myself in the place of the clients. So how could I make it more palatable?"

Business owners who spent sleepless nights worrying about how they would tell their teams about the sale often discovered that their employee attitudes ranged from indifference to genuine happiness for the owner's good fortune. For example, an owner was needlessly worried about a key employee's reaction to the news the business was selling. "The employee said if we didn't sell, he was going to take us out back and beat us up. He said we'd be stupid if we didn't. He didn't have a problem with it. But it was funny."

Another owner said, "When we got done, we actually had people come up and give us a hug and tell us congratulations. We're super excited for you. This is awesome."

Reading in the team does appear to be a greater challenge for smaller companies than larger ones because the relationships in a five-to-ten-person company are much stronger and more intense than in an 80-to-100-person concern. In the larger company, the challenge is the leadership team.

A restaurant owner said, "We brought in pizza, brought in wings. We shut down the restaurant and we just all gathered and I just stood up in front of the group and said, 'It's been such a privilege to work with every single one of you. I'm moving on back to my home state.' I actually had somewhat of a good excuse because back then, my mom was in her 80s, and I kept saying I really need to move back. I need to take care of my mother.'"

She continued, "I think there were surprises. I know there were a few people that, they seemed to be upset because after eleven years with some of them, these were my long-term ones. I've always taken really good care of all my folks. There was plenty of tears by all of us. I said, 'It's been like a great ride, but it's time to move on.'"

Business owners agonize over notifying their team about the sale of the company. In reality, owners should realize that most employees are nonplussed as long as they continue to have a job and benefits.

32: Team Concerns

The stimulus to write a book about the emotions that surround the sale of a business came after advising a business owner who was adamant that the buyer would need to take care of his people. He was 63 and didn't have a child who wanted to take over the second-generation company. Plus, his core managers were near retirement. He worried that if he passed away prematurely, his employees would very quickly be unemployed. Fair enough. In reality, the concern that his rank-and-file employees would all have to file for unemployment if he perished was slightly extreme. Good employees will always find jobs. The decision to sell or not sell a business because employees may not survive without the owner is part ego, part guilt.

It's true that large companies are sometimes acquired in a leveraged buyout because their breakup value is greater than the business as a whole. When this results in employee layoffs, it makes the news. However, this is not a concern for small businesses, which carry little, if any, breakup value. Hollywood promotes the notion of evil buyers who purchase companies to decimate the labor force. This rarely reflects reality.

There are cases where a competitor might purchase a business purely for the assets or customer base. In those cases, some employees might find themselves out of a job. One business owner described such a situation, saying, "We had one very large competitor come to me. They said, 'Why don't we just buy your business?' I said, 'Cool. Show me the money.' And then I asked, 'What are you going to do with my employees?' They said, 'Oh, we're just going to shut it down, we'll just let all the employees go.' I said, 'I'm off the market. I will not do that to my employees.'"

Not everyone feels paternalistic about their teams. When asked about his employees, one business owner laughed, saying, "Are you crazy? Each and every one of my employees has stabbed me in the heart and dragged me through the parking lot at least once." Nevertheless, the business owner made sure his key manager was offered a secure position with the buyer when he sold the company.

Another business owner was blunt. "They have to take care of themselves. When an employee gets tired of working or gets a better offer, what do they do? They call in and say, 'Hey, I'm quitting.

Maybe I want to give you two weeks' notice. Maybe I don't.' They don't give a damn about you."

Buyers will typically try to feel out a seller's hot buttons, and concern for the welfare of their employees is a common one. Buyers will always respond that they will do everything to retain employees, which is true, especially for businesses that utilize highly skilled people.

"Buyers will always declare that they put people first," noted an investment banker. "Of course, they will care for the seller's employees. Besides, what are they going to say? 'We don't like people'? Guys should go into the process knowing this. Don't bank on the buyer's representations. Once, when a buyer made his sales pitch on people, my client pushed back and said, 'I have great employees and I'm not worried about them. They'll be fine as your employees and if you don't treat them good, they'll be fine as someone else's employees.'"

Again, the reality is that, by and large, employees will be fine post-transaction. An owner reported, "We did have a few long-term employees leave, but they were at retirement age anyway and the change in ownership prompted them to make their moves. All other employees stayed and a few took greater roles with the buyer within our region. My nephew, who was slowly being trained to take over the management of the business, is now in charge."

Some owners saw the acquisition of their business by a larger company as an opportunity for their teams and sold them on the potential. "I really cared a lot about my employees," said a business owner. "They came out very good. Everybody was happy going into this thing and everybody was excited about the possibilities with the new owners and continuing to grow our business and prosper."

Nevertheless, business owners often appear to feel guilty when contemplating the sale of their business. It's common. This is why sellers make a point of asking buyers to take care of the employees. Guilt aside, without the hard work, risk, and sacrifices of the owner, the business wouldn't exist. The owner deserves the big payday. He can rest assured that good, well-trained employees will succeed under the new ownership.

"When you're talking about a business, about the emotional side of selling your business," commented a business owner, "some people will say, 'I just want the money, I don't care about anybody.' Then there's people like my sister who really want to take care of all the employees. And I said, 'Seriously? They have to take care of themselves.'"

He continued, describing how he felt he did take care of his people through the years they worked for him. He said, "I took such incredible care of these people. I didn't go around telling them I'm taking great care. I overpaid them, gave them incredible benefits, was so amazingly flexible."

Some business owners worry needlessly about how their employees will be taken care of by buyers. This is a guilt reflex. The truth is that companies acquiring small businesses almost universally desire to retain employees.

GETTING TO CLOSE

Getting to the LOI is not the end. It's halftime. Once the negotiations are complete and the LOI is received, it's time for a CPA and an attorney (both with M&A experience!) to review the document.

Once the LOI is signed, the road is set. The destination ends with the sale of the business. Whether the road is smooth or rocky through due diligence remains to be seen.

"Yeah," said a business owner. "It's almost like the train has left the station and now I'm the passenger. I mean, nothing is done until it is done, but I felt like I had a certain level of commitment at that point."

Another described his feelings. "It was extraordinarily stressful. I realized I've got an opportunity to sell the business for real. There's no question that we're going to sell that. It's real. We have a letter of intent signed. We're no longer kicking tires. I saw the purchase agreement, the assets purchase agreement from the prior company, and they were going to use the same format. It looked good. We'd given them due diligence documents. We had nothing to hide. We'd been completely transparent, as we always are. I didn't see anything to keep it from closing other than the fact that the deal is never done until the deal is done. I'm a strong believer in that. Until they write a check and you sign a contract, it's not real. But I got nervous just because I didn't want to make anything go wrong."

If the transaction fails to close, month after month, it wears on people.' One owner commented about the agony he felt. "About four months in, I knew we were there. There's the hopes and dreams of getting it closed, but you're exhausted. You don't want to just throw in the towel on what you worked on. Every month it just strung along. We finally set a hard date to close December 30. We inked the deal two days before Christmas. He didn't give us a whole lot of reasons for the delays. I think he just didn't get funding. But you just get so sold on this dream you're chasing, right? I've never been divorced, but I imagine if I'd been divorced, that's what it would have felt like."

Buyers can do a lot to ease the anxiety of business owners simply by communicating with them as members of their teams. A business owner commented, "I never once doubted it would happen. The buyer was very optimistic, positive. He really loved my brand and everything about it. He was even talking about how I could really help some other companies he was talking to. He told me I can be a part of this big growth. My continual connection to these guys made it feel like I was part of the team and the in-crowd pretty quick."

For some, the emotions run high throughout the due diligence period. A business owner described hers. "I guess some of the other emotions leading up to it felt like I'm giving my baby away because my husband and I had grown this company. I mean, it was just me and him when we bought it, and now we have a team of 50 people. I felt like, 'All right, I built this business. Here you go. Please don't mess it up.'"

Getting to close is also easier for business owners who use a seller's representative. The representative, whether a banker, advisor, or broker is there to be a buffer for the demands of the buyer during due diligence and to help address and smooth over the bumps along the way.

"Looking at it now, it just seemed like it went smooth," noted a business owner who used an M&A advisor. "I've said that many times to other people. They asked me how the process went, and I say, 'I don't think other transactions go this easy.' To me, overall, it went smooth. I would say for someone wanting to sell, having the right person representing you makes a huge difference. The way things were handled seemed to make it easy. The way things unfolded seemed like it was very easy."

33: Due Diligence

Due diligence is the investigation a reasonable buyer will conduct before completing a transaction with the seller. The LOI is based on a good-faith representation from the seller or his professionals without significant push-back from the buyer. To channel Ronald Reagan on arms negotiations, due diligence is the buyer's effort to "trust, but verify."

"You are going to learn more about your company than you knew, that's for sure," said a business owner. "I did, and I didn't know when it was going to stop. There were times when I thought we were done and then it just got to be more and more. The one good thing is I never hid anything. I always did everything correctly with taxes and stuff, so I felt 100% good on my end, but it did feel as if they were looking to find things."

Another owner said, "It's like having two full-time jobs. You have one job running your business and the other one is selling the company. And I just thought, that can't be true for my little company. It was. The devil is in the detail part of the process. And it was like, 'Okay, I gave you this once. I put it in the data room.' They asked for it again. It was a trying experience reviewing the financials going back five years. It was like a deposition almost, where you're justifying and recounting things that happened years before."

Due diligence always follows an LOI. The buyer will not invest the resources prior to receiving a signed LOI. This means an owner could, mistakenly or deliberately, misrepresent information during the courtship phase, but it will more than likely be discovered during due diligence. Misrepresentations are the greatest reason transactions do not close or are re-negotiated post-LOI.

Due diligence is the most excruciating phase of a business transaction. Sellers can feel as if every nuance of the business is being poked, prodded, investigated and questioned. It weighs on sellers. One said, "The pressure as due diligence progressed was intense, because I wanted this and I wanted it to happen. I didn't play my cards so that they could see that, but I wanted this to be done."

Everyone tells the business owner to gather everything needed for due diligence before beginning the sales process. This is often wishful thinking. The business owner who waits to get everything in order before an intense due diligence will probably never be ready to sell. It's almost impossible to have everything ready, especially for smaller businesses with limited administrative staffs. While it can be done, only one business owner interviewed felt he had everything ready beforehand.

Typical of the business owners interviewed, one said, "The due diligence process, and just the whole process of selling my business, was probably the hardest thing I have ever had to do. It was very, very challenging for me. I knew it was going to be a lot of work. I didn't necessarily know it was going to be *that* much work. It was a very, very challenging time and there was a lot going on."

Another noted, "Due diligence was intense! They audited everything. I mean, from our operating software to our financial statements. They warned us of all the stuff they were going to do, but when they sent me that Excel spreadsheet, which had probably 500 items on it, I was worried I wouldn't get it all done in two months. It just felt like a lot while running a business. But with divide-and-conquer, my partner and I managed to get it done."

For some business owners who have the luxury of operating a larger business with a team (including family members), due diligence can be divided among the personnel. One business owner explained, "So the good news is everybody in our family had different roles to play in the business and I was fairly shielded from due diligence because I ran all the operations. My brothers were the ones who had to take quite a few drinks to get them to mellow out while getting through the process. They were the ones bearing the brunt of the non-stop calls and pulling more data. It was not very fun, even though we had everything set up. Everything was neat and clean and so fairly easy, but it was still a drawn-out process. And the good news is, for me, I was pretty much isolated from it."

The financial demands of due diligence lead some owners to read in their key financial personnel early in the process so they can gain their assistance. "The only people that I brought in ahead of time," said one business owner, "were our controller and our HR director. Those are the only people. We brought the controller in pretty quickly."

It cannot be emphasized enough that, unless the business and purchase amount is so small that the risk is minimal, due diligence is usually the most painful part of a transaction. Buyers, especially sophisticated buyers, demand an overwhelming volume of information. The seller often struggles to keep up.

A business owner described due diligence as "Intense. Intense. We probably had three or four meetings in our office after hours. They had rented some hotel conference rooms a couple times. They had a list of what their CPA firm wanted. They audited everything from our operating software to QuickBooks to the credit cards. Everything! There was never-ending anxiety until the deal closed."

There are cases where the length of due diligence can be minimized. This happens when the seller negotiates a fixed time period, such as two weeks or one month, for due diligence as part of the LOI. Without this constraint, due diligence may drag on for months.

Of course, not all types of business transactions have such heavy due diligence. For example, selling to a competitor who is familiar with the company, and is essentially buying the company to gain the customer list and the employees, results in a lighter due diligence experience.

Sales to employees and family members are also less intense. Insiders don't require the same degree of due diligence and won't take a deep dive like a pure financial or PE buyer would.

The one business owner mentioned earlier, who had virtually everything he needed to satisfy the buyers, said, "I bought a new boat in the process. I was on a sailing trip in the Caribbean in June. And they were going to send me the letter of intent. It just happened to line up while I was out of the country. My claim to fame here is that I signed my letter of intent digitally while under full sail between the islands of Anegada and Tortola. So that's my deal with a cocktail I made. And then two days later we moored at Peter Island. I uploaded 99 due diligence documents to their data portal. I'd already had all that prepared. I mean, I was ready for this."

The owner credited his Vistage group for his preparation. He said, "That's the thing Vistage teaches you. You should be ready to sell your business at all times, should have your stuff in order. They gave me a due diligence list of 99 things they wanted. All I did was rename all the file names to match those 99 items and put them in a thumb drive."

While rare, he was not alone. Another business owner said, "Due diligence, as I've mentioned, was not near as bad as I thought it would be. They were focused on the financials. We had a very good controller. She was really, really good on financials. Anything they asked for, she could pop out a file right away. She'd run a report, print it, print a second copy, and put it in a different folder just in case. I mean, she had paperwork out the yin yang, but the deal was anything they asked for we could produce quickly. So that side of due diligence went well."

Yet the owner still had areas where due diligence was not as smooth as it was on the financial side. He noted, "The technical side was a little more difficult because my head technical person was a little antsy about what her role was going to be in the new combined entity. She was not as helpful as she could have been. Even with her passive-aggressive resistance, we only had about six weeks of due diligence, all in."

Quick and easy due diligence is not the norm. Buyers, especially private equity, perform what amounts to a corporate proctology exam with a never-ending list of requests. Typically, information requested by the buyer is placed in an online "data room." Sellers have questioned the degree to which buyers examine the information sent, with some questioning whether the buyer's analysts are merely checking boxes. Sellers often expressed frustration that requests for certain information often were made more than once.

"They asked for documents I'd already provided," said one business owner. "It was so annoying. Apparently, they didn't know what they did or did not have, so when they made ridiculous requests, I started telling them that they already had it, that it was in the data room, whether I knew if it was in there or not. This caused them to check off whatever box needed checking and they didn't ask for it again."

"All of the due diligence was on my husband's shoulders," said another owner. "He would work all day, and then he would come home and work on due diligence all night, like he was a one-man band trying to pull all of this together for the team. It was so hard for him. It was so much work. And when we did pull the managers over the wall, and said, 'We need your help with these things.' Yes, they would help, but it was still so much work for him, and I was drowning in my new position (outside of the company), so I wasn't that much of a support with him as I had been for so many years. It felt very disjointed. Something that was exciting for me was he was going to get this whole new level of support on a group level. He was going to get an HR team. He was going to get these things that the group could bring that I wasn't there to support him with anymore."

As difficult as due diligence can be, the absence of it can be worse. One business owner ended up with several post-transaction disputes resulting from a buyer being surprised. She believes this wouldn't have happened if the buyer had performed better due diligence. She said, "The guy didn't do hardly any due diligence, which is why we ended up with so many of the problems after the fact. I just assumed that he was confident in his numbers, that he knew what he was doing. Turns out he just didn't know what questions to ask."

Due diligence is a beating, the most difficult part of the sale, but business owners should welcome it. Due diligence protects both the buyer and seller, reducing the potential for disputes down the road.

It's the rare business owner who breezes through due diligence. As a rule, everyone hates due diligence and considers it the most challenging part of the transaction. Business owners can ease the burden of due diligence by bringing in key team members to assist.

34: Deal Falls Through

Some deals fall through. There are myriad reasons why a business marriage might be called off and the bride left at the altar: discoveries during due diligence, the business suffers a downturn, the economy tanks, failure of the buyer to raise the money, or simple interpersonal conflicts.

Outside events can derail a transaction. For example, there was a huge fallout of business transactions after the September 11th attacks. A buyer noted, "I was on the buyside of transactions on 9/11. At that time, I had maybe 10 to 20 transactions on my desk, of which several were under LOI. Not one of these deals ever closed."

The more time a transaction takes, the greater the odds that a problem will arise. An adage of the mergers & acquisitions world is *Time kills deals.*

The news that a sale is off can be devastating, and the closer the deal is to closing, the harder the news is to take. This is tantamount to being told you have an ugly daughter because of your DNA. It feels personal and can arouse anger.

Business owners need to recognize that it isn't the end of the world when a deal falls apart. The owner still has the business. If there was something that ultimately made it unattractive, it can be fixed and taken back to market, possibly commanding a higher price. If the transaction failed due to the buyer, the owner can find another buyer. There are always other buyers.

"We had two deals blow up," a business owner explained. "On one we hit the skid mark. They were probably overpaying for us, so when we hit a two- or three-month period where we were skidding a little bit, it became an excuse for them to back out. The next deal blew up right in the middle of the Silicon Valley Bank thing. They were upfront and broke off the deal right away. Obviously, I was disappointed, but I went through the four stages of grief pretty fast. I said, 'Okay, let's buckle down and get going.' And then we went with a third PE group and everything flew like it should."

Transactions fail to close more often than most people think. "We walked away from a deal 18 to 24 months before the day we finally sold," explained an owner. "We walked away from the first deal on the day of closing. It was mutual. We didn't have our act together. They had some things going on. They didn't need any more

Jacob and Michel

headaches at the time. The buyer and I talked it out, actually. I thought he was going to come in the 11th hour and that just didn't happen. He didn't have the bandwidth to do that."

It turned out to be a blessing for the owner when his first transaction fell apart. He explained, "The first time wasn't near the same money. We sold for 4 ½ times the money that we were going to get from the first buyer. It just didn't feel right the first time. And not to say we were pushed into it, but we felt pushed into it. We doubled our EBITDA the following two years. Some things changed. I bought my dad out. The other owner and I reduced our salaries. We put all that into marketing, expanding the company, and in two years, we got 4 ½ times more. Multiples went up. We had twice the EBITDA."

While business owners shouldn't expect a transaction to fall apart, they can still think through what they would do if worse comes to worst. "I'm a plan ABCD kind of guy," explained one owner. "I never enter into anything without having a backup plan and a backup on that. If you look up the word backup in a dictionary, you will see my name and my picture. I created the word, all six letters. We end up closing on plan E as an elephant. E is how we closed. None of this was the fault of the buyer. These were self-induced problems. There were technical difficulties, legal difficulties, and then who was going to be the trustee? And there's some disagreements between my attorneys and CPAs and myself."

Another owner explains how it's not the end of the world when a deal falls through. He recalled, "We almost sold privately the year before. A consultant we knew had a private buyer. They dragged their feet. The buyer dragged us through the mud for about nine months before he backed out of the deal the week before closing. I said, 'I'll never do this again.' And then a year later, I sold."

Most business owners sign an LOI believing that the transaction will close. It should. If there are serious doubts, owners are advised to pass on the LOI and find another, more stable buyer. Nevertheless, there is always a chance that any deal will fall apart. If it does, owners should take a deep breath. It's not the end of the world. Moreover, the experience and knowledge the owner gained will help with the next suitor.

As close day approaches, transactions can still fall apart. Tensions are high and emotions get charged. One owner described his near miss. "It nearly fell off of the rails because the buyer had gotten so emotionally charged with something and I don't even remember what it was. But he basically questioned my integrity. I spent hours on the phone with my attorney on how to deal with it. In the end, I just said to him, 'I don't like that you said that. That's not who I am. That's not how we operate. I'm going to put that aside as if you didn't say it, because I don't think you meant it. I think it was said out of emotion, and I'm willing to carry this forward.' After the fact, I can't even remember what it was because I literally put it out of my mind."

He added, "Weeks later, the buyer told me after we had that conversation, he called his M&A advisor up nearly in tears and said, 'I think I screwed it up. I called his integrity into question.' The M&A advisor said, 'Oh, my gosh, what do we do?' The buyer said, 'It's in his hands.' And now? I can't even remember what it was. It's gone by the wayside. We're great drinking buddies now. We share IPAs heartily."

The business owner who chooses representation has an advantage when a deal fails. The investment banker or M&A advisor tries to find multiple suitors. Smart sellers' representatives (and almost all of them are smart) will keep alternative buyers in play until the LOI is signed and remain in touch through due diligence until the transaction closes. If Buyer A falls through, the representative will get on the phone to Buyers B and C.

Transactions will fall through. This is where a seller's representative is especially beneficial since he can bring multiple buyers to the table. If one falls through, another will step up. Business owners should accept that sales fall through and other buyers materialize.

35: Quality of Earnings Report

A business owner entering into due diligence may or may not hear the term *quality of earnings (QofE)*. A QofE report is synonymous with due diligence, but it has a slightly different definition. The QofE report reveals the true earnings of a business after recasting the financials to remove anomalies, accounting tricks, discretionary spending, and extraordinary events that skew a business's real bottom line. This information is delivered in a QofE report performed by a third-party accounting firm. The data presented to the buyer during negotiations prior to the LOI should incorporate all the adjustments that would be revealed in a QofE report.

"We had a third-party QofE report prepared," noted a business owner. "It served a couple of purposes. First, it lowered risk. Lower risk justifies a higher price, so the QofE report probably paid for itself ten times over. No, it *easily* paid for itself ten times over and that's conservative."

"Second," the owner continued, "it forced us to get a lot of the material together that we needed for due diligence. Now, due diligence was still a pain in the ass, but without everything we got together for the QofE report it would've been a monumental pain in the ass."

The QofE report may result in adjustments to a company's EBITDA. One owner found that a QofE report increased his EBITDA and value. He said, "We did not tell our internal accounting manager about the sale. So, no one inside the company could do financials, do any financial work. Our CPA firm had an M&A department. We hired the M&A department to do quality of earnings. By doing that, we were able to do a revised EBITDA. We were able to create all those add-backs and all those one-time situations that affected our earnings. We spent hours upon hours on the phone with the CPA firm. They questioned us on every single line item. We went back four years."

Businesses that follow conservative generally accepted accounting practices (GAAP) and do not manipulate earnings will find that a QofE report and due diligence are less stressful and come with few, if any, surprises. This doesn't mean that a business with discretionary or extraordinary expenses can't pass due diligence. It only means that these adjustments must be made.

The QofE report and due diligence will reveal surprises. No one likes surprises, especially surprises that might result in the loss of millions of dollars. Nevertheless, they happen. One business owner received a $100,0000 insurance payout for hurricane damage to his building. The company's bookkeeper incorrectly recorded the $100,000 as income. Because the business owner didn't repair the building before submitting his financial statements to the buyer, the cost to repair the building wasn't factored into the earnings of the business. The earnings of the business were overstated by $100,000. The QofE report caught the mistake. Otherwise, it likely would have been discovered during due diligence. If not, if it was discovered post-transaction but before the holdback period expired, it would have been pulled from escrow.

In another example, a business owner unintentionally misled the buyer regarding customer concentration. The business relied upon two customers for 40% of total sales. During the courtship phase of the negotiations, the owner shot from the hip and reported the customer concentration as 15%. This came out during due diligence and raised concerns with the buyer. The M&A advisor was able to save the sale, but it nearly cost the business owner the transaction. If the owner had paid for a QofE report before putting his business on the market, he likely wouldn't have made this mistake or even been asked the question.

Some businesses engage a CPA to perform an annual audit or review of the financial statements. When this happens, there's a reason. Usually, it's the requirement of a lender or expected by shareholders. A CPA audit is similar to a QofE report in the sense that a third-party professional is looking over the books, giving buyers greater confidence. If a business is unwilling to pay for a QofE report, a third-party CPA audit is the next-best option.

"Our business required a fair amount of bank lending and therefore the bank demanded that we have our CPA perform an annual audit of our financial statements," recalled one business owner. "The side benefit to these audits was that the buyer trusted the audited numbers, so due diligence was less of a grind and there weren't any due diligence surprises."

A quality of earnings report helps business owners prepare for due diligence and lowers the risk of an acquisition, thus raising the price. Business owners should consider investing in a quality of earnings report before going to market.

36: Maintaining Performance

The process of selling a business is distracting, especially during the due diligence period between the LOI and the close. Due diligence typically lasts two to four months, but it might seem as if it goes on forever. Meanwhile, business owners cannot let business performance suffer. This is especially true when the owner attempts to manage due diligence alone, without the help of internal personnel like an operations manager, controller, or bookkeeper.

"I had to pay attention to the trend," said one business owner discussing how he remained focused on performance, "and I had to pay attention to our trailing 12 months because you always hit a bump in the road someplace. And if you can get 12 months that line up really nice, it's a bonus."

Small businesses that rely solely on the focus of the business owner are much more likely to incur a downturn in performance. Since the business is valued based on the expectation of future earnings, buyers observing a downturn may want to renegotiate. Worse, if it appears that the business is experiencing a major downturn, the buyers may walk from the transaction altogether.

Maintaining performance, especially while managing due diligence, is a challenge. Businesses can slip, but they can also recover. One owner said, "We had a rough fourth quarter during due diligence the year before we sold. That was probably the most nerve-wracking part of the deal. There was a huge fear that they were going to try to renegotiate, even in the middle of due diligence. And then, out of nowhere, we had the biggest January in the company's history. And I think it saved our ass. They didn't renegotiate. They held the price of the offer."

"The goal when we went into this," explained a business owner, "was we did not want operations, and definitely did not want any part of our staff, to feel any of the pain of what was going on. A major concern of ours was we didn't want to work so hard to build up this super valuable company only to have everything just break down in the home stretch. We wanted to maintain the trajectory it was on. It worked out well for us. Granted, my partner was pulling his hair out, but I kept mine."

Jacob and Michel

Business owners must keep their businesses operating at high levels during the sales process to avoid the potential for a renegotiation of the purchase price.

37: Stay-On Bonuses

Business owners worry they'll lose employees if they find out the business is for sale. One of the ways to retain employees through the sale of a company is to concretely reassure them of their importance by offering stay-on bonuses.

Stay-on bonuses are most frequently offered to key individuals. For example, a business owner reads in the bookkeeper to help get him through due diligence and offers an attractive bonus at close to keep the bookkeeper from looking for another job before the transaction is complete.

"With the people I read in," explained one business owner, "I did stay-on bonuses that basically said, 'You're going to get me through due diligence and at the closing, I'm going to give you a bonus for doing it.' It was significant. We gave our GM 200 thousand dollars. The controller, the HR manager, and my general manager all had stay-on agreements and they got bonuses at the close of the deal."

Stay-on bonuses can also be offered to the entire team if they're told about the possibility of a sale. Ideally, the owner will get the buyers to fund the stay-on bonus. More sophisticated buyers will balk because they know that few employees leave due to a change of business ownership (though it can be a different story for key employees). Owners concerned about employee retention should be prepared to pay the bonus out of their own pockets (or the proceeds of the transaction).

Surprisingly, across-the-board stay-on bonuses do not need to be significant. Merely paying 500 to a thousand dollars to everyone still around six months after the transaction makes job safety appear tangible, which is all the employees seek.

One seller described his experience. "We wanted to give everyone a stay-on bonus. The guys buying us wouldn't cough up any money, so we paid it out of the sale price. I don't know if it had any impact or not. I do know that everyone stayed with us through due diligence and past the close."

Business owners should consider stay-on bonuses, especially for key people, to keep the team together and functioning well through due diligence.

Jacob and Michel

38: Key Employee Departure

There are cases where a key employee leaves. Owners often panic when this happens, but buyers tend to take employee departures in stride, understanding that this happens in the normal course of business.

One owner confessed, "We lost a key person during the sale period. I thought it was going to hurt more than it did. She was a strong executive with a great resume, so that hurt from a marketing-the-business perspective, but in the end, I don't think it mattered. We found someone else with an even better resume and kept moving forward."

Another owner said, "We lost our controller. He was kind of a nervous cat anyway. He was very smart, but he was really weird. This guy was wacky, but a good controller, very smart. He made some great spreadsheets and stuff. He just couldn't handle the stress. It was no great loss. He just couldn't handle the stress. It ended up being good for me because I saved the stay bonus agreement that I'd signed with him, which was a significant amount."

A business owner talked about losing a key employee during a critical part of due diligence, when the company was struggling to hit its numbers. "I don't know what happened. It was over New Year's weekend and he came back on the 2nd or 3rd of January and just said, 'I can't do this anymore' and quit and went MIA for three days. I was freaking out because this is the worst possible time to lose a key employee. We're in the middle of diligence. But the guy we promoted is still here and doing a great job. So it actually worked out great. But yeah, I was pretty freaked out about that and worried about that affecting the deal."

This is another time when the counsel of a seller's representative served the business owner well. "My advisor said, 'Hey, we got to tell them [about an employee quitting]. Let's downplay it. We've got plenty of people to cover.' And we did. We had somebody in line to at least plug the hole a little. But the buyer didn't freak out. They didn't seem to care."

Where the loss of an employee does hurt is when the employee is a revenue generator. Buyers might try to renegotiate the price down in such an instance.

A business owner who lost a revenue generator said, "We did have a key salesperson whose wife passed away. He kind of drifted off into basically... I don't know, just not wanting to work and stuff." Unfortunately, the loss did impact company performance.

"During the time that we were going through the sale process," noted a business owner, "we lost a key employee, and they had a fit about that. They wanted to renegotiate the sale price, but fortunately, we were able to find someone new. So, in the end, they couldn't reduce what they were paying us. They were just trying to grind us."

Key people leave companies from time to time. It should be no surprise if it happens between LOI and the close of the sale. When it happens, buyers are rarely as upset as owners fear. Business owners should be candid with buyers when a key person leaves and act quickly to replace that person.

Jacob and Michel

39: Coping Methods

Business owners have developed a variety of techniques to deal with the monotony of due diligence. Some made games out of unique terminology used by private equity during the endless calls, keeping score whenever someone said *circle back, bifurcate, runway, bio break,* and so on.

Other owners would focus on things they'd do to reward themselves once they got to close. It could be a major purchase like a boat or plane, an extravagant vacation, or some other goal.

"I'd been casually looking for lakefront property for a couple of years," said a business owner. "During due diligence, I shifted it up a gear, especially during meetings and calls with the PE guys. These calls seemed endless and unproductive. While these guys would drone on, I'd look at real estate listings on my laptop."

Some business owners coped by keeping the endgame in focus. "No, I never felt like pulling the plug and walking," said a business owner. "I knew the payout at the end and I was all in. I'm playing to win. They had this crazy thing called networking capital. I had no clue what that even meant, and I couldn't explain it now. I would call the buyer's CFO. I'd say, 'I don't understand what in the world this is.' She would get on a call and she would explain it again. I don't know how emotional it was. It's just never ending. It was borderline exhausting. What now? What else could you look for? But they kept saying, 'Your financials are so clean. You're one of the cleanest financial companies we've ever dealt with.'"

Due diligence is a grind. If necessary, business owners should come up with creative ways to lighten the mood, handle the stress, and keep the end goal in focus.

40: Second Thoughts

Many business owners have second thoughts as they proceed through the sale. *Am I doing the right thing? Should I wait? What will they do if I sell?* Adding to their uncertainty is the knowledge that, once they sell, there's no going back.

Second thoughts are most likely to appear at the start of the process, at a point when the numbers are all crunched and the after-tax proceeds are less than initially imagined.

The other time for second thoughts is right at the end, when the reality of actually selling is confronted head-on. A last-minute change of heart, especially a goal-line mental meltdown, is disastrous. A private equity investor described a plea to rescind a transaction. "I've had the extreme cases of people who were all-in and on board and didn't have a second thought or a question, and then you get this whole range and litany of emotions and feelings and thought processes. My worst one was when I bought a company on the West Coast. We literally closed. We had a closing dinner after that anticlimactic closing call. Back then, we did them in person. So it was in person. We all went to an early dinner. I jumped on a plane."

He continued, "When I landed, I had 27 missed calls from the former owner. I called him and he is bawling and just crying. Big, huge, manly man. And he was just crying. He said that he had made a huge mistake and his grandfather's rolling over in his grave. I thought, I shouldn't have done it. I told him, 'Listen, you sleep on it tonight. You call me tomorrow. If you still don't want to sell, I'll unwind it, but I want you to take a breath, think about it, and go to sleep.'"

The next morning, the seller still wanted out. The investor noted, "It was early in my career and I was a little bit of a novice. I should have said, 'You have to pay me for everything I paid for the deal.' But I didn't." The PE investor was generous. Rarely will a sale end like this after the documents have been signed.

Backing out of a transaction is the very, very, very rare exception. When asked if they would give back the money to take back their companies, every business owner interviewed said no. As one noted, "I probably had a few second thoughts, but they were quickly extinguished when I looked at the bank account."

Jacob and Michel

Business owners will have second thoughts, but rarely would any be willing to sacrifice the payday to take back their companies. Thus, business owners should balance every second thought with a second thought about the payday.

41: The Close

A business transaction is an emotional roller-coaster ride, even when the process is smooth. Transactions that aren't smooth are absolute white-knuckle events for the seller and the seller's family. Eventually, after all the high emotions, sleepless nights and thoughts that the transaction may never close, it does.

"We're at the top of the roller coaster," recalled a business owner. "It's a done deal. But they're asking questions. They were asking for redundant information, things I gave them four weeks ago. You start thinking, *Did they find something not to their liking?* We were suspicious that they were going to come back and give us another haircut. They didn't. But we were very suspect about some of the motives of these people, these faceless financial people from New York City who were asking some stupid, naive questions."

Once upon a time, before today's modern technology, buyers and sellers met at the seller's lawyer's office to sign off on the volumes of agreements. Today's closes occur over a video call. Signatures are made electronically in advance. These close calls are short. After several months of never-ending ups and downs, the actual close can seem anticlimactic and uneventful.

A business owner described her close. "It's really serious. It's really mundane. They take roll call, hit the button, they send you the money, and we're done."

Closing calls are so undramatic that one business owner wasn't even aware he closed. He said, "I thought it was another one of the innumerable conference calls during due diligence. The CFO asked for some piece of absurd information and I told him I could get it, but it would take me a few days. To my utter shock, he said, 'No, that's all right.' I thought to myself, that's never happened before. Then their attorney spoke up and said something to my attorney. I was wondering why my attorney was on the call and what this call was going to cost me in attorney fees when their attorney said to start the countdown. People started saying congratulations, one after another. I wondered how many people were on the call. When everyone rang off, I asked if anyone was still on the line. Their attorney was. I asked what just happened. He laughed and said I just sold the company. It was so anticlimactic I didn't even realize it."

"Yeah," reported a private equity buyer. "It's very anticlimactic. The emotion I think a lot of people have is one of relief because almost all of their net worth is in the company. And so to not have that risk hanging over you and having cash in your bank account, overall is a good event."

"All the running around had been done already," said another owner. "I was just sitting here with my phone, checking my bank account every 30 minutes to see if the money hit. That's really all that happened."

"So, I'm sitting here and we talked to our investment guy," said another business owner. "We had the account set up to where the money is going into it. I'm sitting here in front of the computer, same computer at the same desk that I'm sitting at now. I'm watching the emails fly back and forth because I assumed we were going to do a video call or something, or we're all going to meet for champagne. And they say, 'No, this is all electronic.' Really? I'm watching emails between my attorney and their attorney. And the buyer's CFO says, 'I've got everything I need.' Their attorney says, 'I've got everything I need.' My attorney says, 'I've got everything I need.' And then the CFO says, 'Great, guys. Congratulations. Transaction complete. Funding will happen within two hours.'"

While the closing event is fast, the lead-up to it may not be. Waiting for the close can be maddening. A business owner described how agonizing it was for him and his partners. He said, "By the time the wire transfer happened on close day, it was a fait accompli. It wasn't like when you're buying a house. 'Did we get the house?' No, this was way past that. It became very procedural in our eyes. 'Are we going to close today?' 'We're going to close Monday.' 'We close Tuesday.' 'Is it going to be in the morning? In the afternoon?' But it was a done deal by that time. And we were just waiting for the shoe to drop. And that felt almost ceremonial."

Despite the anticlimactic nature of the close, closing day still carries a range of emotions. They hit the majority of business owners at funding or in a wave of relief when it sinks in that the owner grabbed the brass ring and offloaded risk.

A business owner described the closing event at his company. "My wife and my partner's wife just showed up here at our office and they quietly snuck a bottle of champagne in. They just came in for support. We got on the call with those guys. It was all video conference. Everything got signed. We'd submitted it. We reviewed it.

They said, everything's good. We released the money, blah, blah, blah. And sure enough, there it is. It pops up in our account a short time later. We just kind of got off the call and there was a lot of tears, lot of hugs, a lot of high fives, a lot of, 'Holy crap, this just happened! Crack open the champagne.' But we were all hiding right here in this office. Just the door shut, and 150 people around us had no idea what was going on."

The business owner whose husband passed away said, "We met at the lawyer's office. We signed all the paperwork. I know that I was very emotional. I'm pretty sure I cried in the car. And then I was running errands and saw a full-size cardboard cutout of Wonder Woman. And I thought, that's how I feel right now. I feel very vulnerable, and yet I also feel very strong. So I took a selfie. I look a hot mess in the selfie. I must have been crying, but I'm smiling. I've got Wonder Woman behind me. I just posted on Facebook and said, 'I did something very brave today.' I didn't give any clue about what that was. I didn't even tell anybody I sold the business for months. But I knew it was incredibly brave for me, and it was a very big emotional step for me to sell the business that my husband and I had built together. And I felt... I knew he was proud of me."

One business owner who built businesses to sell to employees was the most emotional about the close. "The emotions of closing... well, there wasn't a lot of sweetness there. I'm going to be very honest. It was more like a funeral than a party. I congratulated them and I wished them all the best and blessed them. They're good guys to this day. But that did not really alleviate the pain that I was really feeling because of the huge amount of investment that I'd made in that company, in its people. The initial financial contribution, the liability, the weight of all that, and then getting the right people in the right seat, working with the owners and helping develop a sales funnel and then finding the right employees. There was just a lot of work that went into it to get that company birthed and then to see it begin to grow and as a toddler, toddle, then walk, then run, and it was running."

The close is anticlimactic. It is fast. It is mechanical. Most business owners ask themselves, "Is that it?" Business owners should be prepared to be underwhelmed by the close.

Jacob and Michel

42: Funding

Once the close is complete, the next major step in the sale of a business is funding. If the close occurs in the morning, funding usually occurs the same day by wire transfer. If the close is late in the day, funding will likely occur the following business day.

Waiting for funding, even if it's only a few hours, can be maddening. Although there's no doubt the funds will arrive, as the minutes stretch to hours, it's normal for the seller to wonder if something went wrong, to wonder if the money is really going to arrive. In the meantime, it becomes hard to work, hard to think. The seller goes through the day in a type of fog.

Once funding does arrive and the bank account balance has a lot more digits, it's common for business sellers to struggle to grasp the amount. It seems surreal. It can be hard to wrap their heads around the sudden wealth. In truth, the seller's wealth is the same. It just changed forms, from the business to cash.

"I don't know what I felt," said a business owner. "It was kind of disbelief, relief that it was over, and then just wrapping your head around the zeros. I mean, come on, let's be honest. How many people get to see that much money in one place at one time that's theirs?"

"We sold the business," noted a seller, "and it is life-changing money. I think I've done a good job emotionally wrestling with that and managing it. Money does change people. I've seen it. Next thing you know, they're flying all over the place in private jets and acting different than they used to. 'Wow, you're not the same person you were.' I'm hoping I'm not turning into something like that. But, at the same time, there are changes you want to make for the better that you couldn't afford to make before. So, I don't know… It's a tricky one."

The seller wants to tell people about his newfound bounty, but society frowns on people talking openly about wealth. He can't share the information with the people he's worked with all of those years because he feels that tinge of guilt that he's the one who became wealthy. If married, most owners immediately call their spouses, who then experience their own sense of the surreal.

"The call to my wife was… well, we're multimillionaires. It didn't seem real. I mean, it's still just numbers on a phone, right? I didn't bring the money home and was swimming through it or anything. It was just a bunch of ones and zeros on an app. I may have taken a screenshot of it so I didn't have to keep opening the app. I admit, I looked at it quite a bit."

If the business owner was running a profitable business before selling, the proceeds from the sale of that business may not be life-changing. One business owner explained, "Once the wire was done, me and the wife pulled it up on my phone. We looked at it together. We had dreams of buying our forever home. We invested right back into our family. It was assets, investments, and college funds. It didn't sit in the bank account very long, not all of it. But there's quite a bit still in there. There was a sense of disbelief. But when you do what we do, it's very profitable. You can pay yourself two, three, four, five grand a week and then take a 50,000-dollar distribution. Excuse my language, but there's money and then there's F-you money. And I'm not at F-you money. But I can buy quite a bit, except for jets and insane cars. But what can I buy myself now that I couldn't before? There's probably not a big difference. If I want a toy, I can go buy a toy. A new Porsche. I'll go buy a new Porsche. Even before I sold, I could have done it because we were making enough money. So I don't think life changed in that way."

Another seller described the emotions he felt at funding. "It hit me. It was the same emotion that I had when I walked my first daughter down the aisle and gave her to that strange boy at the end. At that point, I have no control. I have influence, but I don't have control. And I was standing here crying like a baby, just sobbing. And my brother walked in and looked at me, said, 'What the heck's wrong with you?'"

He continued. "It was a very emotional day. We grew this thing from nothing. Three brothers starting in a garage. And the blood, the sweat, the tears, the firing Mom and making Dad retire. And punching holes in the walls and yelling at each other and growing it up to where it supported our families. It was a very, very emotional day. I just sobbed. And even a couple days after, when we started telling vendors and suppliers, people would say, 'There's something different about you.' I just kind of had a loss of words."

This was not the only business owner to draw an analogy between the business and children. Another said, "It's a happy goodbye, selling your small business, because you're celebrating it. At the same time, you're mourning it. It's like empty-nest syndrome. You want your kids to grow up, get married, leave the nest, go on, thrive. And yet when they do, people have a total identity crisis. Suddenly, it's who am I without my kids at home? And it can lead to grief and depression if you don't really identify and work through that difficult transition."

Funding is not the end of the story. It's merely the end of one chapter and the start of the next.

Funding follows the close and it's a completely different event. Most business owners feel overwhelmed when confronted with the number of digits in the account balance. Business owners should simply enjoy the moment.

43: Relief

When owners were asked what they felt after selling their businesses, the most common response was *relief.*

Relief means different things to different people, but usually revolves around the reduction of risk or the removal of stress. The difference between the two is subtle. While risk provides stress, the risk reduction is usually financially related, such as paying off a loan, avoiding a downturn in the business cycle, avoiding future litigation, and so on.

Stress often deals with the day-to-day demands of running a small business. It's usually people-related, such as the stress of keeping customers happy or the stress of dealing with prima donna employees.

Many owners felt that running a business was a high-wire act. Yes, they were on center stage, but one misstep could cause everything to fall apart. As the business became more successful, the stakes became greater. Most business owners seemed to harbor a certain amount of imposter syndrome. They worried that their success was more due to luck and circumstance than effort and acumen.

"I have imposter syndrome," said a business owner. "I had imposter syndrome when I started. I had imposter syndrome when I sold. I have imposter syndrome now. I always wondered, *When does the rug get pulled out?* I realize everything I did right was just dumb luck."

One owner said, "It was relief after it was gone. My greatest fear was that it would end up being worth nothing because I would kick the bucket and the kids wouldn't know how to run it and the thing would just go down the tubes."

"The best part of the sale for me," said a business owner, "was not worrying about a gazillion details. First thing in the morning, I would check my phone to see who's not coming in today. That kind of thing. Whether or not we had enough work and can keep everybody busy. It's a business that goes from lazy to crazy in 24 hours and back again. I no longer have 40 people depending on me for their paychecks. So that's the best part of it, not having that worry."

When she closed, another owner said she felt, "Excitement. Relief. We got it done. I can move on with my life. This is going to be great. That's how I felt."

Some business owners also expressed relief because the process was over after they had harbored doubts that they would ever close.

"It was stressful," said an owner about the period between the LOI and close. "You don't know it's going to close until it closes. Until you're paid. I am a positive guy, but you have to think about everything, and the uncertainty of the deal closing was one thing that kind of was scary."

"All I got was relief," confessed another business owner. "I don't have to worry about going to the bank and pulling down my underwear and giving them all my stuff just so I can get the promise of a loan that they're going to overcharge me for, and then have to use it, and then worry about paying it back. When you got a million dollars out there and you're on your last 100,000 dollars, living week-to-week on payroll. That's a bad feeling."

Eliminating concerns about payroll does appear to be the source of relief for many business owners. One said, "For my entire adult life, every day I would look at the cash balance of my business in anticipation of the next payroll. Every day. Looking back now that I am out of the business and retired, the greatest relief is that I no longer have to worry about cash balances in the business."

"Before we sold the business, we swept our cash out and distributed it," recalled another owner. "There was minimal operating funds left in the business. A week before payroll, the parent company asked us to wire them a bunch of cash. Okay. Whatever. It's their money. I didn't think about payroll when we did it. Then, the morning of payroll, I was driving to the office in a near panic. Did we have enough in the bank to cover payroll? Where could I lay my hands on some more money fast? Then it hit me: It wasn't my responsibility. The parent company had to make payroll. Whoosh. I felt this wave of anxiety flow from my body. At that point I felt incredible relief."

The most common feeling after the exit is relief… the process is over, the risk is over, the obligation is over, the stress is over. Business owners should take a deep breath and feel good that they have accomplished such a major achievement, one that most people will never attain or understand.

44. Owner Rewards

After close, some business owners sought ways to reward themselves. Many, who felt uncomfortable taking vacations while running their businesses, made up for lost time. Some traveled for as long as three years. Others made major purchases. Yet most did little or nothing.

One seller described a list he had assembled of places he wanted to see after he sold his professional practice. He said, "I got certified in scuba and we went to Belize. We swam with the sharks. Scuba diving has been one of the most peaceful, relaxing things I've ever done. You're down there and your thoughts are somewhere else. Of course, fishing there is good. Italy, last year, was so amazing. I've never taken more than a two-week vacation, and we were gone 16 days, and it wasn't enough. It was just that relaxing because I didn't have to worry about the clinic."

Another former owner rewarded himself with a car project. He said, "I've got a Shelby Cobra Daytona coupe kit that I'm building from scratch. Number one, it's keeping me busy and out of my wife's hair. Number two, hell yeah, it's a reward. To build my car and stuff, we put 150 grand in my own checking account."

"I had an uncle that I respected," recalled another seller. "He was my favorite uncle. Whenever he bought a car he would pay cash. He'd say, 'These people who buy all this stuff on credit, they're going to get in trouble one day.' And I'm sitting there paying my credit card bill every month. When I sold the company, I said, 'I'm going to buy a car and I'm going to pay cash, just like my uncle Ben. And I went with a check and I bought a car. That was my treat."

The sale of a business is one of life's major accomplishments. Building the company, taking it to market, enduring due diligence, and closing the transaction are worth celebrating. However, some business owners were very conservative about how they celebrated.

"We didn't do much," one seller remarked. "I think we had some champagne. That was about it. The next day was just another day at the office. In fact, we didn't even buy anything extravagant. One of my college buddies who went on to law school said to me, 'You shouldn't buy anything for a year. Make sure you're comfortable with the money you have.' I thought that was pretty good advice."

This wasn't the only business owner who received this advice. Another said, "I got some advice that I actually didn't follow at the end, but a couple people told me, 'Don't buy anything. Don't go freaking nuts for a year.' Just Vistage advice. I had another guy in my industry tell me that, too. He's said, 'Don't do something crazy right out of the gate. Don't go buy a Ferrari or whatever.'"

The owner did buy a second home. He said, "I rented a house two hours away at 7,000 feet. It's 25 degrees cooler in the summer, and it's an easy getaway from here. I rented a house for about a month in August, six months after the transaction. We were there for about four nights. And my wife said, 'We should get a house here.' I said, 'Yes, we should.' So we started looking and we bought one. I waited six months."

One owner rewarded his children but not himself. He said, "I could have whatever car I wanted. I could drive an Aston Martin if I want to, but I have more pride in driving a Ford Explorer with 435,000 miles on it than I would in a 175,000-dollar Aston Martin. But I do love the fact that my kids can drive a Range Rover and the new Bronco and a Jeep. They can drive 50,000-dollar cars that I wasn't able to and make sure they have an appreciation for what they have. When my kids turned sweet 16, we got one a Cartier ring, which I don't know anything about. I was three blocks from the trailer park growing up, so I don't know anything about Cartier rings, but it's a 1,800-dollar gold ring that kids covet these days. My oldest daughter had diamond stud earrings for her sweet 16."

The majority of owners did little. Many went out to a celebratory dinner. The next day, they went to work.

Some owners reward themselves for enduring due diligence and closing the transaction, but it's often modest because successful business owners tend to be personally conservative. Sellers should be careful about making major expenditures for a year following the sale of their businesses, but feel free to reward themselves with a toy or trip if desired.

45: Team Rewards

Some business owners rewarded their entire teams after selling. Others only rewarded their key people. And still others didn't do anything. There are no right or wrong choices. Each owner had a different outlook and a different situation.

Among those who rewarded key employees, generosity tended to increase with the sale price of the business. Transactions involving smaller valuations simply may not offer the business owner the luxury of rewarding employees.

"I paid all of them something," said a veterinarian. "Even the kennel boy got paid something. I'd tell them, 'Hey, guys, I appreciate everything you did,' and just gave them a check. I just thought it was the right thing to do."

Rewarding everyone does happen, but it's not the norm. An owner said, "My partner took his first key employee out to dinner. I took my first key hire out to dinner separately. We broke it to them. I ended up writing a personal check. It was Christmas time, right? So, I wrote both of them a personal check as a thank you. Not out of company funds, but out of what I had earned and took them to a really nice steak dinner."

Another owner noted, "The people who were with me early on and helped build the business all got lucrative rewards at close. Two of them were mid-six figures. Another was seven figures."

The owner of a larger transaction noted, "I spent more than a couple million dollars with the broker. I gave away 6.5 million dollars to my team because they earned it and deserved it."

Another seller recalled, "I gave our marketing director 100 grand, gave another manager 40 grand. Gave my ops guy — and just because he was such a dick and just did things on his own time frame — he only got 40 grand or 60 grand maybe. It varied. It was just completely discretional. It ended up being almost a million and a half or something that we gave to people. That helped ease my wife's guilt of, 'Oh, we made all this money and these poor people are going to work for some greedy national company.' It was kind of cheap to buy that off."

One owner said, "They offered me stock. I said, 'Hey, that's well and good, but let's work on those numbers on the stock, because I want to take part of my stock and give some to my leadership team because they need to have ownership in this company.' They actually said, 'That's brilliant. We agree 100%. Let's do that.' And so we rounded up the stock value to make sure that my leadership team had kind of skin in the game."

"We paid every employee something when we sold," recalled another seller. "My Vistage coach calls it 'sleep-at-night money.' Can you go to bed every night and feel good about what you did for your people? I think we gave every employee 500 dollars per year that they worked for the company. It was a bunch of money. We had guys that worked for us for three months and we gave them 500 dollars."

He explained how he arrived at the 500-dollar number. He said, "It was like trying to decide what to do and where to cut it off. I quit doing it and just said, let's just pay everybody. It's not a lot of money in the big scheme of things, but it was a lot of money. I met with every employee individually. I met with all the people who had worked for us for like 25 to 35 years individually before we transacted. A lot of those people were influencers in our company. I told them what was going on, thanked them for everything they did, and handed them an envelope. They didn't open it. And then they got home and they opened the envelope and there's a 15-thousand-dollar check. They're texting me and going, 'Holy...'"

The impact of the checks he wrote was significant. There are lessons for buyers who might consider building some kind of acquisition bonus to those who will become *their* employees after the sale. The owner who distributed the 500-doller-per-year checks said, "Their attitude changed dramatically, from 'I hope it goes okay. I've heard horror stories. I'll stay as long as it's good.' Other employees were going to them, saying, 'Oh my God, can you believe this?' Those guys were a calming influence on the rest of the team."

Even if they rewarded all of their employees, some owners still felt guilt over their windfall, recognizing that business is a team sport. They didn't really do it on their own. Lots of people helped. Nevertheless, most owners founded their businesses. The businesses would not exist without them. Purchased or inherited businesses, likewise, would not have reached a similar point without their owners' involvement. Any guilt is societal and unwarranted. Owners should recognize that they assumed the risk and, while their teams helped, they were compensated along the way. If the business had failed, no one would have offered to share in the loss.

Rewarding the team is not a requirement. Some business owners feel no need. In some cases, the limited amount of money in a transaction does not allow the seller to be generous. In other cases, rewards serve as a kind of guilt indulgence, easing the consciences of the owners who paid them.

Rewards to the team upon the sale of the business are varied. Some reward key employees. Others reward everyone. And some, not at all. Business sellers should reward people in a way that satisfies their consciences and leaves no regrets.

46. Taxes

There is no escaping death or taxes. With the sale of a business, a large tax bill will come due. Even knowing the amount of the tax liability before the close of the business, the sheer size of it can be stunning when it hits.

Tax planning, including changing the legal structure of the corporation, has the potential to reduce the liability. This must be executed well in advance of the close date. Owners should consult a CPA and/or tax attorney before taking such action.

"My tax bill was a slap in the face but it wasn't a shock," noted a former owner. He was philosophical about the liability. "You still got it. You got to pay it. It means you made a lot of money. It's a good thing. You can't do a hell of a lot about it. You can strategize and plan and do the best thing you can. I don't try and get too wound up about stuff that I just can't change that much."

"Honestly, paying taxes was just a cost of doing business at that point," said another seller. "We talked about everything we could to minimize it. But the accountant said, 'You're gonna pay a big bill. You're gonna pay more to Uncle Sam than you ever paid in your life. Welcome to paying your fair share.' I think that is exactly how he said it. Yeah, my fair share."

"We built a bond ladder for taxes," one seller noted. "We were prepared for them. It was the government's money but we damn well maximized it as long as it was in our hands and due payable to them. When it came due, we just paid it. We made money on it while we had it. The taxes were a given. You're not going to be investing what you sold your company for. Start about 60% conservatively. I always err conservatively that way. For my state, with total capital gains, it's right at... figure 60%. We made money on the other 40% for the six months we had it before the government got it. What are you going to say about a tax bill like that? It hurt. I felt like Elon Musk for half a second there."

The sale price of a business is not the after-tax value. One seller said, "It sounds great... We're going to sell our company for 20 million dollars. Well, by the time taxes and buying some assets out, employee stock appreciation, and other stuff, it starts chipping away. It's 15 million dollars really fast. It sounds great, selling your company for 15 million dollars, but what you really need to do is get 20 million

The Business-Exit Roller Coaster

to just get to the 15. And I think a lot of people underestimate that. I did. The tax check sucks. I didn't like writing it, but I didn't lose any sleep over it. We knew very early on that's what it was going to be. That's the price of poker. I could buy another house somewhere else for the tax check, but that's not reality."

As surprising as it seems, some sellers failed to account for taxes. They had to scramble to come up with the funds to pay the government. In one case, paying taxes meant selling real estate acquired after the close.

A buyer cautioned, "People should be very aware of the tax implications. Most people don't think about it until all of a sudden, it's that, 'Oh, crap' moment. There's work that can be done prior to a sale, levers that can be pulled, and avenues to save huge numbers in paying taxes if the right paperwork is in place and you have the right legal advice and tax advice."

Another buyer commented on how some business owners failed to properly account for their total tax liability. He said, "I have had times where people were disappointed. They thought the sale price would be treated all in capital gains, but actually part of it was capital gains and part of it was regular income and they came back to renegotiate. I've definitely had that scenario happen where people were disappointed. I've never had anybody not close, but I've had people clearly disappointed in what they ended up with."

Even when the money is set aside, some business owners do not feel that this is merely their obligation. They weigh the value received from the government through the years against the taxes paid and find the value short. Some are fatalistic about it. Others are angry.

"Some business owners are just pissed off," explained a buyer. "They're mad at the government, mad at life. They think, 'I worked my whole life building this. Why is it fair for them to get to take so much in taxes?' We get a lot of Democrats who turn into Republicans during that process."

"I went on a text rant to my kids," confessed one seller. "I told them what the tax bill was for that year. It was millions, *millions*. I divided the bill among them and told them this is their money, their inheritance that just went down the government drain."

Another seller commented on the tax bill, stating, "Yeah, it was frustrating. I mean, it's not like I didn't pay taxes along the way. I paid lots of taxes every year on income, on property, on assets, on sales, on employees, on everything. It seems like that should be enough, but then there's capital gains. Uncle Sam is your silent partner who had his hand out when you do well, but is nowhere to be found if you flop. I guess I should count my blessings I don't live in a state like California where the state grabs another 10 or 15%."

Capital gains seem to stand out because of the size of the tax liability. Business owners are wise to have their CPAs calculate the tax liability and immediately set the funds aside in an interest-bearing account. This lessens the shock and the owner can focus on the larger, after-tax remainder. The taxes may seem high, but the amount retained is the greater number.

No matter how prepared, the sheer size of the tax bill can be stunning. It's worse for business owners unprepared for the government's take from the sale of a business. Business owners should plan for taxes, set aside the money, and conservatively put that money to work until tax day.

IV

WINDING DOWN

The wind-down from the sale of a business can be as short as a matter of weeks or it can last for years. The wind-down really lasts as long as any non-compete and non-solicitation agreements remain in effect. It is the post-game for the sale of a business.

The wind-down is different for owners who choose to stay on and become employees. Not every buyer desires this, but most buyers will want the owner to remain on the payroll for a while to ease the transition. Also, buyers want to squeeze as much tribal knowledge out of the owner as possible.

To keep owners motivated, buyers will often utilize an earn-out, which the owner receives if certain performance targets are achieved. Some owners remain only as long as the earn-out is in play.

For owners who stay on, becoming a subordinate in an organization where they once called the shots can be a challenge. It still feels like their business when they stay on, but it's not. It belongs to someone else and the former owner must learn to accept, implement, and publicly support decisions he may not agree with. This can be the greatest challenge a seller faces.

"They don't need my position," noted a former owner. "They don't need a CEO or principal over here because I can't bill anything out. What can I bill out at my hourly rate? I can't work on projects. I've become the face of the company, if you will. I'm the community relations guy. I do some business development. I have brought in some business, and that's what I try to do every day. And then I mentor employees. Yesterday I had three one-on-ones with different employees about stuff, and I've had two more today. But they don't need that. I don't want to say it's not productive. It is. It is useful, but it's not what they want to pay for."

Jacob and Michel

47: Staying On

Few business owners who choose to stay on and become employees last more than two years. Too many years of self-employment seem to make people unemployable. They chafe under directives from others, disagree with management decisions, and resent the rules and procedures imposed by the new owners. While there are exceptions, someone who has only been accountable to himself for decades is not likely to settle in as a good employee.

"Most companies," said a former owner, "when they buy a business, they're going to want the owner to stick around for a while and do something to contribute towards the success of the business. I guess if you really are not ready to retire totally, I can see how you might want to stay involved. I didn't do that with my business. Didn't really want to. People often ask me, 'Why don't you just keep part of that business?'"

"I never considered selling and walking away," said another former owner. "My attorney said I was the exception to the rule that he never sees. And if somebody does stay on, he says they never stay on more than a year."

One business owner who stayed on described his experience. "I sat at my same desk with no employees reporting to me, but with a fancy title. I was expected to do whatever I could to help the business grow by training people who were in the business."

Oddly, the potential to get fired frightened one owner. It's odd because he became financially independent upon the close of his transaction. He said, "I woke up two weeks after we had sold. I woke up in the middle of the night sweating. I thought, I could get fired tomorrow and not have a job. What would I do with myself? I was actually more paranoid about that than anything. But even if that happened, we're okay. We could live the rest of our lives financially."

The possibility of getting fired crossed another former owner's mind for slightly different reasons. "These jackwagons zeroed out our PTOs. Maybe we should have negotiated it, but no one thought about it. I'd been working my ass off for the better part of a year to get through the sale. I needed to decompress. I booked a trip to Europe with my wife, told my staff, but didn't tell the buyer. Every morning in Europe, I got up early and cleared out email. I probably over-communicated. I kinda worried that this might be a firing

163

offense if they found out. But my attitude was, so what? If they fired me in the first couple of years they'd have to pay me 12 months of severance. That wouldn't be so bad."

An M&A advisor said, "I coach my clients to understand that, despite the hype and excitement about continuing to run the business post-transaction, they should be prepared for life after the business. It's okay to plan on continued employment post-transaction, but be realistic and prepared for life after that if you turn out to be a lousy employee."

After the transaction closes, the seller and buyer undergo a honeymoon period. The buyer typically imposes few rules at first. During due diligence, many buyers claim that they don't plan to change anything. For a while, this is true. The seller is treated almost like an important customer.

At this point, the seller is enthusiastic. If purchased by a larger entity, he gets invited to corporate meetings where he gets to see how a larger organization operates. He revels in the freedom that comes from his newly realized lack of risk. Things are exciting and fun.

A seller still in the honeymoon period described the excitement. She said, "There's excitement about what's next for us. There's definitely a lot of opportunity and a lot of opportunity to do our own thing as well. My husband is still excited. He's got a whole new leadership team to work with and people who believe in him and believe in our company and want to make us the model. So, there will still be a lot of excitement for quite some time."

Over the next few months, most sellers see the honeymoon fading. Human resources is typically the first area to be integrated, followed by information technology and/or finance/accounting. The parent company begins to irritate and even enrage the seller. He disagrees with business practices, especially overhead allocation. He loses control of his P&L. Finally, a day comes when something sets him over the edge. It might even be something relatively minor, like a dispute on an expense report. He feels his anger building, looks at his bank account, and concludes that he doesn't need this anymore.

A seller who stayed on attempted to explain his life under private equity. He said, "My benefits went up in cost. My insurance costs went up. They would decide for you on the amount they would spend on marketing. They did a lot of trial-and-error marketing. They spent a ton of money in marketing. At one time, marketing percent was over 10. More money, less results. Just throw money at this. They make deals for vehicles, and they would just show up on my lot. They would tell me, 'These are your two vehicles. You have to pay for them.' Well, I don't need them. I don't want them. They would say, 'You're gonna take them. We made the deal for them, so you get two of them.' I said, 'I don't want them.' They wouldn't listen. They don't care who I am. They won't listen to me. They don't value my opinion."

While the owner struggled working for private equity, he did appreciate the money he received. He said, "The transaction was great. The money was fantastic. I love the fact that I can do what I want, when I want, and the financial freedom. But my daughter said, 'The only good thing about this was the money. And I hope you enjoy it.' I said, 'Well, part of it's going to be yours eventually, so you're welcome.' But the only good thing about this *was* the money. This did not get a better experience for my people. I had better benefits. I had better buying power. The best thing about this was the money. That's reality."

Even when somewhat disillusioned, a seller might continue to operate his company if the incentives are right. One owner-turned-employee said, "They wanted us to stay on as operators, and then they gifted us management-incentive shares, which is what keeps me in the seat on a regular basis. Because if it wasn't for them, I don't know that I would be here."

Another former owner thought the ideal length of time to stay on was a few months. He said, "I think two to three months would have been the magic time. It's enough time to deal with your employees after the announcement. Take away the fear factor of all the employees. Talk through the reasoning with all your people. Make the introductions of the leaders to the PE company or the buying firm. Get them in touch with the right people. Then they start going, and say, 'Hey, what if we do this?' Okay, I'm out. Hey, what if we took the marketing? Okay, that's when we should have left. Sure, take it. But I'm not going to be here to deal with it."

Most business owners should be prepared to be asked to stay on after the sale of their companies, but should not expect to stay long.

48: Focusing on Strengths

Business owners who stayed on after the sale and experienced the least frustrations were those who played to their strengths. They did the work and activities where they found enjoyment and where they excelled.

"I became a sales trainer for their sales reps," noted one former owner. "They wanted me to take the knowledge I'd gained over the past 30 years and impart it to their sales force. So I traveled around the country dealing with franchisees and their corporate branches."

He added, "I was not running the business. That was part of the deal. I was out of the weeds totally. I was not the manager of my operation… from day one. They had my right-hand man. He became the VP of operations of the newly formed division. Then they gave me free rein. I got to go out into the marketplace and interview companies and identify technology and software that could facilitate the sales process. I did what I wanted to do. I developed my own programs. It was really exciting and fun. I was making a nice big salary and it was a pretty good deal. There was no reason for me to leave."

Business owners who want to play to their strengths must be proactive. Another former owner reported, "I reached a point after the business was sold where I took everything I didn't like to do and either delegated it or hired someone to do it for me. I worked on what I wanted to work on. I used it as an opportunity for self-development and self-actualization. You know Maslow's pyramid? Well, I lived in the apex, self-actualizing and having fun."

This requires a change in the mindset. First, there's a sharp recognition on the part of the seller that he, indeed, no longer owns the company. Many people who stay on after the sale have a hard time mentally letting go. A sense of freedom comes with the acceptance that the seller not only does not call all of the shots, but responsibility belongs to others. Instead of responsibility for the entire organization, he's responsible for his own performance and actions. This makes it easier to deal with, if not easier to accept, decisions he disagrees with.

The ability to take the detached view seems to come more easily to former owners who had a prior corporate background with a large company than it does to those whose entire careers were working in small or family businesses. For the former Fortune 500 employee, returning to his old role is like putting on an old suit. It may not fit quite as well, but it's still familiar.

Another former owner said, "I let the glamour of the corporate life make me think it was going to be easy. The one thing it has taught me is, it doesn't matter who owns it. It's not easy if you own it, but if you're private equity owned, it is really not easy."

He described how he got away from his strengths, saying, "You have to stay focused. For me, it's that daily cadence that makes the business successful. And that's the number-one thing I got away from. I got away from the fundamentals."

As a result, the business struggled, but he took personal responsibility, refocused on his strengths, righted the ship, and consequently operates with a fair amount of freedom. He remarked, "I was pissed off that I allowed it to fail. Now it's fixed. It's running well. No one is going to mess with me because I'm running at 16% EBITDA in a company where most of the general managers are falling apart because they're not entrepreneurs. They don't know how to drive a machine. Corporate is trying to take people and put them in GM roles, and that only works if you have a very solid regional GM, which they don't. They don't know how to hire the GMs either. I don't know how long I will stay. As long as it's fun, I'll stay. Maybe three years. Maybe 18 months. But if I keep having the freedom I have, I'll stay, because at this point, they pay me to just make sure the machine stays running."

A near universal strength of successful business owners is decisiveness. They built successful enterprises because they were comfortable making decisions that involved company investments, employees, and customers. After they sell, there's a tendency for some owners to hesitate before making a decision. Since it's no longer their money, they stop to seek approval from the buyer before acting. They should avoid abdicating decision-making, hesitating to make the financial decisions that they used to make with ease. Yes, they've turned over control. Yes, they're now playing with someone else's money. If this makes them uncomfortable, they should clarify their level of empowerment. Does the buyer want them to make spending decisions ranging from property leases to ordering inventory to capital equipment purchases?

Hesitation and delay are not healthy for a business. Owners should recognize that they're kept on because they made good decisions in the past to build their businesses and make them attractive to buyers.

Buyers want them to continue to grow their companies. Decision-making is a strength. Owners should play to their strengths, seeking clarification about any limits.

With the reduction of risk and responsibility following the sale of a company, former owners can and should focus on activities where they excel and draw enjoyment.

49: Learning Opportunities

Another approach to making a successful transition from owner to employee is to look at everything as a learning opportunity. Like focusing on strengths, this requires the ability to mentally relinquish the notion of total responsibility for the organization.

For former owners who lack experience in a larger corporate environment, this appears to be an effective approach to surviving in the new role of employee. This is especially true if the seller is relatively young and apt to start another business in the future. It's an opportunity to watch how a larger company operates. It helps the once and future business owner get a better idea of how to scale up a company.

A former owner explained his experience, saying, "The journey over the last 18 months with the PE group has been fun. I got asked to be on the CEO council. There's five CEOs who meet with the executive team once a quarter. I'm learning about private equity and how they run companies and how they are positioning for the turn. It's just a different mindset. It's interesting and fun, too."

He continued, "I suppose something bad could happen and I could get frustrated and quit, but right now I'm happy, still challenged, still energized. I also think we're very fortunate that we're with the PE group we are. The synergy has been really good. They do business the right way. There's a bunch of other groups where I probably wouldn't be working anymore."

The PE group also afforded the former owner the chance to perform his own acquisitions, which may have always been available to him, but was something he had never tried. He said, "We just did a tuck-in of about a 1.2 million-dollar business. It was an interesting learning experience. How do you take an outside company and make it into part of our business? It's gone pretty well. There's a few hiccups in anything you do, but so far, it's worked out great. That was an education too, and fun. A challenge we hadn't done before."

Aside from observing the corporate planning process, human resources, IT, finance, and so on, the odds are good that the larger company offers in-house training opportunities that the seller can leverage. He can also attend outside seminars and conferences that he might have been reluctant to utilize when he ran the show because of the cost, time away, or concern that his team would perceive this as slacking on his part.

Additional learning opportunities may come from the greater resources a larger company provides. For example, one former owner utilized a business coach provided by the buyer. He said, "There was a guy there who was a business coach the parent company hired and at a certain level you could get access to him. Some of the businesspeople I respected had positive experiences with coaches, so I thought about what I could do with the coach for self-development. I also wanted help with the issues of working with a parent company and navigating the environment. The coach had good business and psychological advice, plus he offered intimate knowledge about the parent. It absolutely helped me grow as a businessperson. Sometimes you just need someone else's perspective."

For the entrepreneur who attended the university of hard knocks, staying represents an opportunity for the advanced business training that you otherwise only get from an MBA. It allows former owners to grow personally and professionally. And, for a very rare few, they might discover a new role they can enthusiastically embrace: building a second career working for the buyer.

"How many of my peers have sold?" asked a seller who intended to start a new company when his non-compete expired. "How many of them have gone and got the further education that we get while working for private equity? How many of us now understand how these multiples work? How many of us are going to have a pocket full of money? Now I get to see how to do acquisitions. I get to see all these different things."

Former owners who lack large-company experience should approach staying on as an opportunity to observe and learn how larger businesses operate and scale.

50: Corporate Suits

Some buyers are from the same industry as their acquisitions. Others are not. This is particularly true with private equity buyers. A number of sellers in the latter situation commented with disdain about the new owners showing up and presuming to have superior business knowledge (after all, buyers seem to reason, the owner sold to them). Many commented that the suits do not look or sound like entrepreneurs, noting that they were "different" beyond the skinny jeans and puffy-vest comments noted earlier. It's not a problem at first, but it becomes one over time if conflict between the seller and buyer arises.

Arrogance is not limited to the corporate suits. Former owners, especially if they are entrepreneurs, may be impeded by their own arrogance and disdain for people who are good with a spreadsheet but possess little line experience. The former owner must recognize that no matter how well he's run his business in the past, he might have much to learn from the buyer's personnel.

Intimidation also goes two ways. "Our general manager was intimidated by us," said a former owner. "First, he's a small person and we physically intimidated him, as weird as that is. But also, we knew our business and industry intimately. He was insecure and felt like he had to come in and be in charge, instructing us and telling us what we needed to do instead of collaborating. So there was knowledge intimidation in addition to the physical intimidation. He was also younger and had less education and experience. When we got into a meeting with him, he was dealing with two people who he couldn't match up with intellectually. He kept trying to go around us because he was intimidated. Finally, there was a degree of financial intimidation. He was dealing with two guys who are financially independent and he needs his salary."

Another factor is the new and foreign world of corporate politics. Politics may be present in any organization, but business owners, by nature of their positions alone, are largely immune to them. They may have to manage the politics among subordinates, but not the gamesmanship of a superior or peer.

A former owner who was promoted to a position as a regional general manager explained how his naivete about corporate politics ultimately cost him. "Corporate had been basically running this one operation for 18 months in advance of me taking it over. And they're the ones who ran it into the ground. The financial backers came on site, talking to their CEO. He asked me what I was going to do to fix the operation because it was the black eye of the group. And I told him, fix the pricing, fix the marketing, fix the systems and processes, get it back to the right ratio of revenue-producing employees to office workers, and just get all the things correct. And he said, 'Well, you make that sound so easy.' I said, 'It is.' The CEO was sitting there, and after seeing his face and thinking back about it later, that's where I screwed up. I put egg on all of their faces… Everybody at corporate. So now I had a target on my back."

Another former owner commented on his first frustrating interaction with corporate politics. "You're on a GM call because at this time there are 30 brands. When you're on a GM call, the first time that you hear the CEO is unhappy with your performance is when he calls you out in front of 30 people and says, well, if it wasn't for these four brands we would be performing well and be able to recapitalize and sell. But these brands are dragging us down."

Fundamentally, the issue appears to be one of perceived arrogance. One former owner explained in colorful language, "So this guy showed up at a trade show during due diligence and hung out in our booth. I asked him what he was going to say if a prospect asked him about our products. He said, 'Don't worry. I know the products as well as you do by this point.' Really? This effing kid didn't know jack. He didn't know our effing customers. He thought he did. He didn't. If he talked with anyone, he was either going to piss them off or look like an idiot. But you couldn't tell him that."

That, in a nutshell, captures the arrogance of the corporate suits. People who build multi-million-dollar businesses are being told how to run them by twenty-somethings and thirty-somethings who may have been born after the owner started his company.

One former owner shared his frustration, which was echoed by several others. He said, "The delusion that private equity has any clue how to run my business is gone. These guys are number counters. They're bean counters. They don't care. I decided to stay as far away from these people as I could. They are not my friends. We are unequally yoked. Scripture talks about being unequally yoked to someone. You are unequally yoked with private equity because your goals aren't aligned. Because my goal is to build a brand that provides a great opportunity for my people and for my community, that provides a valuable service so we can all win together. Their job is to print money. That's all they care about."

Most former owners seemed to feel that their influence and autonomy waned over time. One discussed how the relationship with his direct superior soured fairly quickly. "I call him up with an idea and initially it was pretty agreeable. Initially it was, 'Yeah, good idea. If you feel that's the right thing to do, go ahead.' And I think, nice. All right. Guess we'll just keep the status of business as usual. That quickly changed within about two months."

Another talked about conflict with the buyer. He said, "We sat down with the consultant right after close and talked to her about my role. She said they didn't have me in a day-to-day role, that my job was to block and tackle for my team. That probably got me in trouble. I was being the daddy bear. I was protecting my team. It probably got me sideways with the buyers. But guess what? I still work there and they still use me as a referral and they don't bother me. Most importantly, they don't bother me. They said, 'You come in one day a week and we're happy.' That was such a relief for me because I don't know how I would do with that corporate monthly meeting. Why'd it suck this month? Because it sucked. What didn't you do? I don't know. Yeah, that would be tough."

These sentiments are not universal. Some former owners are surprised by the degree the buyer leaves them alone post-transaction. One said, "I'm looking out the window every couple days, wondering if they're ever going to show up and say hi. Are they ever going to knock on the door? Is anybody ever going to call me? Just crickets. We're just doing what we do."

Of course, this is not the norm. If the buyer is private equity, acquisitions may largely be left alone while the PE acquisition team is consumed with the hunt for new businesses to buy. Once the target numbers are hit, attention shifts to the companies purchased.

Former owners should be prepared for, though not expect, a certain degree of arrogance from buyers who are steeped in finance but not in their business operations.

51: Reports and Meetings

Business owners have certainly experienced meetings, but they were always in charge. Now they are merely seats around the table. Plus, they are required to produce reports to the parent or buyer. The guy who was always in charge is now subservient, which inevitably grates. If the meeting is perceived to be a waste of time, what initially irritates eventually begins to infuriate.

Some of this is simply the governance that a larger company requires. If the owner, now employee, believes the reporting is beneficial to his understanding of his business, he's unlikely to object. It's another story if the report is perceived to be a report for reporting's sake.

"There were some things that I expected and some that were kind of unexpected," recalled a business owner about new management. "Some of the stuff, like tracking vacation days and having to go in an online portal to register your vacation, get it approved by three different people, and all this stuff, is a lot of malarkey. But I guess you got to do it that way with an 800-person company and 600 of them are in the oil field."

In part, this is a conflict over the best use of time. As a rule, business owners want to move the needle. The corporate managers want to measure and track needles. Both are needed, but conflict can arise when corporate personnel pull the former business owner away from customers.

One former owner described his frustration with the meetings his new superiors required. He said, "I'm an old-school guy. It's all relationships. It's all people. It's all culture for me. My boss is an MBA. It's all finance for him. He wants to see the P&L. He wants to see the sales reports. He wants to go through pipeline meetings with me and do all this other stuff when I need to be in front of the customer."

One former owner confessed, "We had these quarterly reports we had to send in. At first, each required a big dog-and-pony show. Then we just emailed them. Then I began to question whether anyone read them. Finally, I filed one with all kinds of sarcasm in the copy like, 'Here are numbers, blah, blah, blah, though we have no faith in the accuracy of these numbers due to the erroneous financials we're provided.' If anyone really read the reports, I expected to hear about it, get called on the carpet about it. Crickets. This was busy work. Screw that. I quit sending them. More crickets."

Another business owner said, "I started going to regular meetings, which were pretty boring. The paperwork load was enormous. All of a sudden, I found myself doing reports. Of course, they're a publicly traded company. We were privately held. They were doing reports that were a necessity in Canada. I had one person we really needed to fire. My boss said, 'Oh, man, we don't want to pay that bill yet. Let's give them another chance.' I said, 'Pay what bill?' He said, 'Oh, gosh. We'd have to give him two years. Two years' salary. That's our policy here in Canada.' What? I had a lot of that going on."

For the first time, the former business owner may be required to fill out an expense report. No longer can he just charge everything on the company card and pay it off. He must now track and identify. While he might understand the need, he still will not like it.

There are some positives. Meetings that involve the former owners of other companies acquired by the parent are generally well-received. It's lonely at the top, and business leaders who ran their companies largely in isolation for years welcome the opportunity to mix with other business leaders.

These types of peer meetings seem to occur in organizations with a smaller number of subsidiaries. If the number grows, the in-person meetings tend to fall by the wayside, likely due to the greater expense and coordination requirements.

Meetings and reports are part and parcel of a more bureaucratic operation. Larger operations, especially those assembling subsidiary operations, are, by nature, more bureaucratic. Business owners should accept them and remember they are receiving a paycheck to attend them.

52: Buyer Decisions

Business owners who are accustomed to making all the decisions, or at least to having veto power, must cede ultimate decision-making when they sell their businesses. Intellectually understanding this and emotionally accepting it are very different things. Most former owners struggle.

Inevitably, there will be decisions the former owner disagrees with. Sometimes, these are minor annoyances. Sometimes, they're significant.

When it's a sale to private equity, the former owner should view the decision process with an eye towards timing. It may have taken him 30 years to grow his business, but the PE managers are operating it on a three- to five-year timetable. This changes the approach to many decisions. PE is going to upset a few apple carts because the funds don't have time to wait.

In addition, the new owners likely have dedicated professionals for things like information technology who will impose rules and restrictions the sellers may resent, but must ultimately accept.

In some cases, the former owner must also adjust to layers of management above him. While he still may run his operation, the separation from the top creates a feeling of insignificance.

"At one point in my career, I worked for a Fortune 500 company in a mid-level engineering position. The CEO was four levels above me," noted one former owner. "After I sold, I was still running my business as a subsidiary president, but the CEO was five levels up. And this was definitely not a Fortune 500 company. I've got a really solid business track record and far more experience than anyone I reported to up the line to the CEO. No one cared. No one wanted my opinion, insight, or experience even when it affected my operation. I felt like I didn't really matter."

Former owners who felt like their input didn't matter were often the most frustrated. As one said, "The company stresses 'people first,' which couldn't be further from the truth. It's board members first. I was even on the board. We didn't even get to vote for the shareholder stuff. I talked to the attorneys. They said, 'Yep, as long as they went down the line and got enough votes to get an approval, they didn't even need to ask you. They just needed to tell you what they were doing as a board member.' So I said, screw this. I'm off the board. I'm out of the company, and don't call me again."

The frustration grows when the former owner feels like he's watching a preventable car wreck or, as one described it, an airplane crash in real time. "If you're flying in a plane and you're watching somebody flying to the side of a mountain and you know how to fix it and say, 'Hey, pull up. Hey, hey, jackass, pull up on the yoke and don't run into that mountain.' And he won't listen. Well, that's the hard part because ego and emotions are the biggest thing."

Another former owner who walked away upon the sale of his company shrugged. "It's their business," he said. "I got my money. They can do what they want."

This was echoed by another former owner who was coached by an M&A advisor. "My advisor told me early on in the process that one of the problems he sees a lot of is a guy will come to him crying about how they're ruining his business and he has to have a long conversation with them about whose business it is. He asks, 'Did the check clear?' If the check cleared, he asks, 'Whose business is it, really? Okay, now why are you getting upset?' And I took that to heart. I mean, I've used that in some conversations with the buyers. Dude, it's your business."

"It's their business now, not mine," said another. "It's like selling your house. The buyer can paint it pink and that's their decision, not yours."

And yet, many former owners felt it was their obligation to give their advice when they saw the buyer making a mistake. Maybe the buyer would listen. Maybe he would not. Yet, by offering the benefit of their business acumen, they felt like they fulfilled their fiduciary responsibility. On occasion, they would push back if they felt it important enough, though they still might fold.

"Our controller quit," said a former owner. "With the things the parent pulled into corporate, it was hard to justify a full-time bean counter in-house. The parent's CFO wanted us to use part of an accountant on his staff. This wasn't a hill to die on, so I didn't fight it. In hindsight, maybe I should have."

Sellers who stayed on and resisted what they felt were bad decisions generally had a more difficult time. When their frustration became too much to handle, they quit. "I finally just told them I've had enough of you playing your game. You can have somebody else come play it. If you're not going to listen to me, why am I here? I'm the regional president. I'm the GM. I can't make a budget. I can't make hiring and firing decisions. I can't make all these decisions. Why am I here? Y'all are going to run it in the ground. They didn't listen to me. Some days I don't think they could even understand how I ran a business without them."

Despite this former owner's frustration, he's not critical of private equity as a whole. He explained, "I have friends who are part of private equity that lets them run their show. They have to have the same six or seven core things in place. Other than that, it's theirs to operate and run. They don't hear anything unless there's a bad month. They have three bad months in a row, then corporate may step in. Other than that, they're running it and that's the way it should be. These Harvard Business School, Notre Dame business school, whatever graduates don't know how to run these companies."

"It's not all fun," noted another former owner, "but what did you think you were going to get? We have 47 brands and there's guys who just complain about all kinds of things. What the hell did you think was going to happen when you sold? You gave up control of your company and you got a big check that's sitting in your bank. I don't know why people don't connect those two things. You just gave up the right to be the boss."

One of the advantages of making a clean break is avoiding the challenge of accepting decisions you disagree with. "My husband stayed on. They wanted him to stay on two weeks to a month just to acclimate them. He did that for about two weeks. He was really glad to just leave it because he saw them doing things that weren't the way we dealt with things, and they weren't going to listen to what had worked for us. They wanted to make their own way, so it was best to just let it go. And after two weeks, he just came home and said, 'Enough is enough. I'm done.'"

One bitter former owner said, "I stood up in front of my employees and said to them, 'I know you don't like this, because change is never comfortable.' And I lied to my own employees. I said, 'You will be better off a year from today than you are today.' And they were not. They were not better off a year later. They were hassled by the corporate people. My executive assistant asked, 'Are they trying to make me quit? Because I will.' Eighty percent of my people had worked for me longer than 15 years. Within two years, they drove off all but three. Buyers shouldn't BS people … because they're going lose what they bought. And I feel that by driving my employees away, they lost a lot of what they bought."

Former owners should be prepared to accept and support decisions they might disagree with after selling and staying on. However, this is not the universal experience. A business owner who was in a strong personal financial position before selling and who sold to an employee praised the new owner. He said, "The energy that he has! He's doing things much better than I did as far as managing the company because he's putting the time and effort into it. But he's got to pay the note. So maybe that makes it different. Maybe if I hadn't been in the financial position I'm in, I'd have felt differently and I'd have worked a little different. I want this person to succeed. I want the continuation of the company to be successful. I want to go to a restaurant and have somebody say that we're still doing a good job for them."

When two partners stay on after the sale, they seem to have an easier time coping with their new role as subordinates. If there's a need to push back against a management decision, a partner can provide confirmation to the other that it's the right decision. The presence of a partner as a sounding board also reduces the chance that a relatively insignificant issue that happens on the wrong day will blow up into a reason for prematurely walking away from the business. Each partner serves as a form of pressure-relief valve for the other. Each gives the other someone to vent to. Each can offer the other needed perspective. When necessary, one can talk the other off the cliff.

Buyers will make decisions former owners disagree with. The business owner should remember, it's no longer his company.

53: Time to Leave

As previously noted, few business owners who stay on last long. The buyer's purpose in keeping them is that the former owner provides continuity for the business and makes the transition from the previous ownership to the new owner smoother. Yet there will inevitably be a time when it's necessary to separate.

Splitting from a business that a person owned, if not also started, is not emotionally easy. It's been described as a corporate divorce. Leaving a business that the person loved and grew for years, or even decades, can be a wrenching experience.

Another analogy that was used was that staying on is like watching a child go to college. The child is growing up and away. The child is still not independent of the parent, but that day is coming. When it comes, the parent watches the child or business follow its own course, independently. One former owner explained, "It was like this for me. When my son graduated from college, got a job, and moved out of the house for good, he became self-sufficient. He didn't need me and his mother anymore. While there will always be a connection to us, he was pursuing his own life and his own goals. They weren't necessarily the same as the goals we had for him and we had to accept that. When I sold the business and it came time for me to leave the company, it was similar. I'd done the best I could to set the business up for long-term success, but it wasn't up to me anymore. Just like my son wasn't in my control — and shouldn't be — the business wasn't in my control. I will always love my son. And I will always love my company. But now, in both cases, I'm just an observer."

When a child graduates from college, it's expected and planned. How does anyone know when it's time for a business to graduate from his stewardship? There were several ways former owners knew.

Some knew because the new owner told them. They may not have been ready to walk away, but the new business owners were ready for them to leave. "They gave me a six-month contract and said I can stay on for six months continually. After the first 30 days, I knew this was going to be six months and no more than that. So I stayed six months and left. And it was three months into it when my boss came up to me and said, 'We're going to just let this six-month agreement run its course and you'll be gone at the end of that six-month period.' I said, 'Thank you. I'll be happy to do that.'"

It's generally not a surprise when the new owners want the founder to leave. One said, "I had seen the writing on the wall for about six months prior where they were saying, 'I don't really need you involved anymore.'"

Another said, "They made it pretty clear to me when their first guys came in. I still didn't know what to say. Did they want me around? Did they not want me around? What were my plans? How often did I work? And they made it clear to me that day, if I only wanted to come in a day or two a week, that'd be fine with them. So they made it pretty clear right from the get-go that I wasn't needed. I was okay with it. I was happy. Actually, that's kind of what I wanted out of the deal, but I always tiptoed around it. I had the team in place. They did not have to replace me."

Others feel hamstrung by the bureaucracy. Used to calling their own shots and no longer able to, some former owners become frustrated. It reaches a crescendo when something pushes them over the edge. Financially independent, they walk.

"I think it wasn't immediate," said a former owner about his recognition that it was time to leave. "They were pretty good with me. They said, you just kind of run your thing over there and you're doing great, except for this one thing, except for this second thing, except for this fifth thing. Pretty soon it's like you've been assimilated into the Borg. After two and a half to three years, there's a growing list of things that I would not do this way. And sooner or later, it kind of got to that point where it's not worth doing it."

An equal number left when they became accustomed to their new financial status, accepted they had more choices in life than ever, and wanted to spend their days pursuing time with family, travel, volunteer work, and simply enjoying their wealth. "I'm 61," noted one former owner, "and I just feel like I'm 25 until I wake up in the morning and all of a sudden, I'm sore. I just wanted to be able to enjoy life. I think I was smart enough to know that there's going to come a day that the body's going to change. Your mind's going to change. An old boy told me one time, there's no headstone in America that says, I wish I'd have spent more time at work. And that's kind of what I live by."

Another former owner said, "I've got money in my pocket and I don't have the fear of pissing people off and losing my job at age 50. So I had a good time with it for a good, solid year. And then the next year was just laborious. Nobody gave a damn what I did, so I just kind of stayed under the radar and did what bad employees do. I was doing exactly what they asked me to do, but nothing more. I was ready to move on. I was at that point."

One woman described how her husband came to realize it was time to leave. "The buyer would let him work for as long as he wanted to, but it took him just about six months to figure out that the buyer didn't need him anymore. The company was running just fine without him, and we had taken pains to train some people ... to take over for us. So, it could have run even if we decided to retire but not sell."

Suddenly realizing it was over and that it was time to leave is common. It's like a switch gets flipped. When it happens and the owner mentally disconnects and mentally separates from his old business, it's relief. It's a reduction of stress. It's a new day, a new world, as one put it. "I did make the decision to leave when we were down in Florida for a month. This was something I had never done in my life. That's when I kind of came to that decision of, I'm done! The goal is changing, and it's time to move on. And that's when I called and had that conversation with them about, I'll give you till May. And it was like a new world, man. Just the stress. The stress just goes away."

Another described the process he went through to understand it was time. He said, "I kind of had the realization that this is where I was trying to get to. Why am I still doing this? Why am I still fighting for this goal I can't ever really get to? It's kind of like having a baby, your first baby. When you're in your twenties, you're never really ready. You think if we buy the house, we'll be ready to have a kid. But you're never really ready to have that first kid. Eventually you just got to do it. And that's kind of where I was. I'm never really going to be ready to leave. I just need to get the hell out."

He went on to describe how he put together a solid team of middle managers and the only person missing was a general manager. Once the GM was in place, he knew it was time. "The GM started and it's been a different me ever since. I'm mentally ready. I've accepted it. It's not my company. I need to stop trying to solve all of the problems. It's their problems to solve. If I can be helpful, then great. If not, I'm not going to stress out over it."

Sometimes, people simply do not want to leave. They can't envision doing anything different than what they've done for years or decades. One former owner talked about his desire to stay on and how his wife didn't understand. "My wife really, really was pressuring me to lay off, to not work so much. Me leaving was the hard part, which we still haven't dealt with, quite honestly. She would ask, 'Why are you doing this? Why are you still getting up at 5:30 in the morning to go to work?' I just kept blowing it off because I didn't want to deal with it. I don't think it was fear of losing my identity or any of that. I think it was just habit. This is what I did for 30-plus years. This is all I've ever known. This is what I do. She didn't really understand that. We didn't address it. The pressure was constantly there. 'What are you doing? You're stupid. Why are you getting up? You don't need to get up. Go do something fun.' She didn't understand that this was fun."

Timing factors can also affect when a former owner chooses to leave. Typically, these involve incentives put in place by the buyer, namely earn-outs or other operating incentives. Without question, chasing an earn-out does seem to keep former owners fully engaged.

Sooner or later, it will be time to walk away. Business owners will conclude this on their own, or the buyers will conclude it for them.

54: Walking Away

Eventually, the former owner who stays on does walk away. While some did cartwheels out the door, most were unprepared for the stark reality that the company, which had been such an important part of their lives, is gone. They might have thought they were ready, but it still hits hard. "That first year, my husband was more emotional than I was. He had a lot more into it because it was his dream. I came along as a support system. I certainly had a lot of feelings about it because I wanted it to be successful and I'd put a lot into it. But he was the one really tied to it. So it's a lot harder for him to kind of let go of it."

When former owners finally walk away, many struggle with a loss of identity and with finding purpose in life. Depression is more common than one might think. A business owner who was interviewed on his last day, while packing up his office, said, "It actually isn't as bad as I thought it would be. It's surprisingly uneventful. Packing stuff up was... I was good with that. Probably the hardest thing was the people. Just this morning, my service manager walked by. He'd been with me for about 15 years. He was crying and gave me a hug. That was tough. Another manager walked in to get the key to something or other. He's this big guy and says, 'Man, I gotta go. I'm getting emotional.' It's just crazy."

He continued, "I can even remember thinking, *It's not my company. It's not my responsibility to solve all the problems. It's their company. They're the ones who need to solve this.* Yeah. I knew the logic. I had already thought about it, but it took cutting the emotional connection to go. It's not your problem, dude. You gotta go."

Once he made the emotional disconnect, he said, "There was a change. There was a definite change in my whole demeanor. It was almost like an I-don't-give-a-damn attitude. But I didn't let it come out. I was very careful not to. It definitely felt that I had a new mission. My mission was to assist in any way I can, but I'm not the one responsible anymore."

"My last day was... I don't know how to describe it," recalled another former owner. "It'd been announced for weeks and I'd had the date circled for months. I want to say it was like locking up your house after a relocation, but it wasn't like that. On a relocation, you're focused on the next house, next city, next job. I turned in my keys, key card, and walked out the door. I was overwhelmed by this empty feeling. It was like this hole opened up and swallowed me. I tried to think about the money. I tried to tell myself that now I can do anything I want. But all I felt was empty."

Leaving a business isn't hard for everyone. One former owner said, "I was thrilled. The final day, my son, his wife, and the grandkids all came. They were so excited for us. I couldn't wait to get out of there. My son still talks about it. He says, 'Mom just threw everything in the back of the truck and said, let's go.' I kind of did. I was just so glad to leave there. And it was not that I didn't enjoy it. I love nothing more than what I did. I loved the paperwork. I loved working with the customers. I did all the bookkeeping. It was a really heavy load that I carried, but I just knew it was time."

Another left after six days. She said, "I was in the office for six days after the close. After six days, I said, there's no value for me being here. Call me if you need anything. I was on the payroll for six months."

It seems that the day a business owner agrees to stay on is the day he should begin to prepare to walk away. One owner confessed, "For the longest time, I couldn't imagine I would ever want to quit working. I liked the intellectual challenges. I liked the people. But as I got older and I didn't need the money anymore and I got this corporate overlord, it wasn't as much fun. I realized leaving would still be a big challenge so I talked with a counselor. He had me do some exercises to help envision leaving the company. That helped me. Then there were the plans about what I needed to do to leave the legacy behind I wanted. All in all, it took about 18 months, but I was ready when the time came."

Actually walking away, leaving a business that an owner built and ran, is easy for some and difficult for others. Owners should be prepared for an emotional day.

55: Retirement Parties

Some businesses throw retirement parties for business owners. These are usually good-faith efforts to give the owner and team some closure. Whether they are positive or not is an open question.

A retirement dinner was a positive for one owner, who said, "The employees wrote a lot of nice things, had a dinner. My favorite thing was they gave me a Mepps lure that was engraved with *The legend has retired.* And then the flip side, it says, *Gone fishing.* And then there were ornaments. This was in May, but they still gave me some ornaments and other things. People ask me, if you had to do something over again, what would you do? I said, I should have been a cowboy, so they gave me a *Should have been a cowboy* shirt.

One owner was adamant there would be no celebration after he attended one of these events. He said, "I flew out to a customer's retirement party. I had more than one motive. I wanted to show John some appreciation. I also wanted to retain the business as a customer after the ownership change. There was lots of food. A number of long-time employees offered tributes or roasts. And John was miserable. He was uncomfortable with the whole show. It all looked too forced to me. I decided I would never do something like that. If I wanted a retirement party, it would be me and my wife in Europe."

Another seemed to feel the lack of a retirement party denied him a sense of closure. He said, "The day we closed on the sale, our wives made plans. We got a limo down to the waterfront, had dinner, rooftop bar, came home. That was it. Other than that, it's been very uneventful, very non-ceremonious. They didn't have a retirement party for me. They didn't. There was no balloons and cake. I'm going to walk out the door, I'm not coming to work anymore. It's just going to be another day. Get in the car, drive off. It's weird. That is weird."

Whether a retirement party is welcome is largely dependent on the business owner's attitude. Some welcome them, even need them. Others couldn't care less. The takeaway? Owners should make their feelings known.

Some business owners want the closure of a "retirement party" event. Others dread it. Business owners should let their teams know before leaving.

56: Loss of Identity

A business becomes part of a business owner's identity. It's how the business owner identifies himself. It's who he is. When he sells, it feels like he's selling himself, selling his soul, selling his identity. The day after he walks away, he no longer knows who he is. He loses his identity.

Owning a business is "just like any addiction," noted one owner. "Definitely that was the case for me. Looking back, I tried so many times to create that margin of separation, but I jumped back into it. And there's multiple reasons for that. The business was an emotional thing for me. I got a lot of purpose out of it. There's a lot of identity tied to it. Although I didn't really realize that until after I sold."

Another said, "That was my business. That was what I did. Right? And I stayed on for a while, but when I walked away from it, it was kind of like I'm going through this loss of identity. You don't really have that loss of identify because you have multiple identities. Okay, I lose that one, I've got all these. Does that make sense?"

For one business owner, the stark reality of no longer having a role in, or being a part of, a multi-generational business was terrifying. She didn't even know how to introduce herself. She said, "My entire professional career, since I was 21 years old, I worked at the company. It was my identity. I spent the first 20, 30 years being my mother's daughter, and then I spent the last ten years being my daughter's mom because I really developed my daughter."

She continued, "I was a force of nature in my industry. Anytime I entered, I met people. I introduced myself anywhere. It doesn't matter what it was. I was associated with my company. My company changed the way America eats. We had an amazing culture. I was in *Time* magazine. I was in *People* magazine. I was in *Nation's Business*. I was in the *Wall Street Journal*. I was in *Inc!* magazine. I was in *Fast Company*. I was in *Fortune*. I mean, I'd done this my entire career."

To figure out how to introduce herself, she turned to a friend who is a business coach. She said, "I had one confidant friend who had run public companies. She ran a giant public company and now advises and serves on half a dozen boards. I called her up one day and said, 'When people ask me what I do, what do I say?' She said to just develop a script. What do I say? I'm not a stupid person, but literally, when you're caught up in that whole process and you've spent 45 years with one identity, how do you transition? She said, 'This is what you say, something like this: I spent the last 45 years owning and growing my family business. I changed the way America eats fruits and vegetables. My company is responsible for introducing more than 200 new fruits and vegetables to American consumers. Our brand was in every single supermarket. I'm happy to say that in January of 2023, I had an exit, a successful exit. Now I'm taking a well-deserved sabbatical. And who knows what the next chapter holds?' So that was my script. So once she said that to me, I thought I can say that. I just relaxed thinking about that."

"For me," another commented, "I've been working since I was 15. I could not bring myself to say the 'R' word—retirement. But I didn't know what to tell people. What the hell was I?"

Other former owners shunned the term *retirement*. "I've been begging my wife to stop telling people I'm retiring. I'm not retiring. I'm reloading. That's the word I chose. It doesn't make sense to most people, but I like guns, so that's the word I fabricated. I need to just stop. I need to pause, I need to reload, re-aim, and then we'll start firing. Oh, what do you do for a living? Well, I'm a former business owner. And now I'm reloading. I'm reloading to find my next venture."

The loss of identity can be devastating. One former owner described the impact it made on one of his partners. He said, "Doug wouldn't let it go emotionally. It haunted him for almost a year. It was the equivalent of taking away his identity. I'm a faith-grounded person. For me, this whole thing's been a different journey than my partners, who are not faith-based. And Doug's identity was tied up in the business. He really struggled, to the point where he was not functional. It affected his relationships. It affected him to this day."

Of course, not every business owner takes their identify from the business. One said, "My identity wasn't attached to my business. I feel like, for me, entrepreneurship is a tool to build wealth, not an identity. A lot of the dentists say that dentistry is their identity. I didn't feel that way. My identity is me."

Towards the end of the research for this book, a fascinating correlation was recognized. Extroverts were more likely to tie their identities to their businesses. Introverts had less of an issue. A self-proclaimed introvert said, "I'm worried a little bit that I'll lose my connectivity in the whole industry, but not losing my identity in what I do. I'm pretty confident in myself. I know who I am."

Many business owners have a good part of their identity wrapped up in their businesses. When they leave, they lose part of themselves. They should prepare by determining how they will describe themselves and introduce themselves to others after they sell.

57: New Purpose

As difficult as owners find it to let go, the larger challenge from walking away is filling the void created when the business is no longer a part of their lives. Business owners, by nature, are purpose-driven people. It's an essential aspect of their success. The business is a driving purpose in their lives. With the sale of the company, the purpose is gone. Unless they give careful thought to replacing the business purpose with one of equal or near equal meaning, owners will struggle to find fulfillment once they walk away.

A dentist who sold his practice said, "All those dentists that are exiting their practices and find financial freedom, they have no clue what to do with themselves or what they even want."

Another owner said, "Our purpose for building that company was gone when it was sold. We planned to sell the business, but didn't plan on what we were going to do after we sold the business. I know we should have thought about it. People should think about what they're going to do once they sold."

"The lack of purpose hit hard. I had a really hard year," said a recent seller, "and I don't know that anybody necessarily knew how tough it was."

"Selling the company was more of a big first goal in life that had been achieved," said a relatively young former owner. "I think that was the disappointment. Can I get back to that goal again? Can I go achieve the next big goal? That's the fear. Did I just finish what I can do? And now I'm going to be put out to pasture? I don't care if I was 40 years old. You still have that fear. Am I good enough to do it again?"

"I just keep finding projects to do around the house," said another seller. "But the projects are going to run out and then what? Then what do I do? I can't just sit. Like my wife said to me today, I do more now and I get more exercise now. That's good, but she made a comment this morning. She said that I wouldn't know what to do if I woke up in the morning and didn't have a plan on what I was doing that day. She is right. I have to have a plan. I have to know what I'm doing today. I just can't go fishing for the day, it's not who I am. I have to have a purpose."

The sense of loss can be significant. Another former owner said, "You just lose the sense of purpose. That's probably the biggest one for me. What is my purpose now? There's not a company to take care of. I don't have to worry about employees. I don't really have to worry about kids or grandkids or anything like that. So, what is my new purpose in life?"

It is important to have a plan. However, the plan should include a purpose that is worthy of the owner. If the plan and purpose fall short, an emptiness will remain.

"You still have stuff to offer. You still have contributions you want to make, and you still will. You need that goal. You need that purpose, and if you have not found it yet, I get it. I've been struggling as well," confessed a former owner.

The importance of the purpose a business provides cannot be stressed enough. An owner explained how the business gave him meaning. He said, "I saw the business do cool stuff for people. I saw it do cool stuff for my team. I saw it do cool stuff for the community. It fed me in a lot of ways. It gave me a huge purpose in a lot of good, good ways."

A former owner who found a new sense of purpose explained it, saying, "Right now, I'm doing exactly what I think I was meant to do. All the training that I had, whether it's biochemistry or pharmacology, I'm applying that to the supplements now. I'm actually running a clinical study. I've always been interested in clinical studies because I've had to speak using them as evidence. But now I know how they run because I'm running this one, and it's run just like a drug study."

Business owners should work on their purpose before they sell. One said, "I think you need to start planning for that. It doesn't matter if you're 70, 60, 50, or 80. You need to start thinking about what you're going to do or what you want to do. If you had X amount of ability, money, whatever, health, whatever it is. Put your dreams down on paper, just like you do goals. Go after them. Don't sit back and just say, I'm 70, so I'm going to croak now, because you probably will."

The attitude a business owner takes can make a huge difference. "I'm still learning," said one about the period after the sale. "The past year and a half of this process has caused me to grow and learn more about myself more than anything else in my life."

It may seem that business owners are one-dimensional. Some may indeed be that way, but the vast majority have more than one purpose. "We have God as a purpose. Of course we do," added one owner. Outside of faith, there's family, friends, and hobbies. However, these have existed alongside the business and are not likely to fill the void when the business purpose ends.

When the business owner is more multi-dimensional, finding a purpose is easier. "I wasn't worried about who I'd be or what I'd do because I did so much volunteering with the Rotary and with the state trade organization. I wasn't worried about staying busy because I had worn so many hats through the years with all my volunteering. I would be content being at home and was actually relishing the idea of really diving into some projects to keep me busy."

It's difficult for busy owners to think about a new purpose when enmeshed in day-to-day business activities, let alone going through the added demands of selling the company. A healthy approach is to spend the first days and months after walking away on finding a new purpose. One explained, "My goal is, I'm taking the rest of this year off to decompress. I need to separate myself from the business. I need to break those habits of waking up and doing the same morning routine that I've done for 30 years and driving to the office. I need to break those habits. I need new ones. I'm a big believer in purpose. I got a couple of books I've been reading about purpose. I'm looking to identify what I'm going to spend the next half of my life doing."

When staying on with the buyer, former owners postpone the need for a new purpose. One who did this said, "A couple of old sages that are in my life said, 'When you're done, something will come. The opportunity will present itself for you to do something else. I don't want to be boots on the ground anywhere. I could sit in a couple of meetings a year and give advice. Maybe I could go coach football at high school just for fun. I don't know. I love to cook, so maybe find something doing that. I don't think I want to own a restaurant."

Another said purpose came as a revelation after walking away. "I knew what I wanted to do. I could tell it felt right. What felt right was to do executive coaching. So I had hired a web designer. I bought my domain name. I had to get a website developed. I had to develop a logo. All those little tiny, unimportant things. But when you're going to be in business you have to have a business card and a logo and all that kind of stuff."

Here again, there appeared to be a split between introverts and extroverts. The former seemed to have an easier time finding a purpose to fulfil themselves after walking away. Perhaps it's because they're more introspective and satisfied with hobbies and solo activities.

Business owners need to identify a new purpose for themselves after they walk away. They risk facing a sense of loss and emptiness if they don't.

58: Depression

Business owners who sell receive a big payday. In many cases, they receive life-changing wealth. They can afford almost anything they want. Yet, giving witness to the idiom that money can't buy happiness, it's not unusual for a former owner to become depressed.

A popular goal-setting technique is the "Wheel of Life," in which an individual's life is broken up into six to eight areas, such as financial, family, health, community, spiritual, career, and so on. People are encouraged to round out their lives. Using a balloon as an example. When it's pressed on one side, it expands elsewhere. When it's placed in a box and pressed, it's more likely to burst because there is no room to expand. The squeezed balloon is a metaphor for an out-of-balance life. For example, a mother who lives almost solely for her children might be devastated when they move out. The mother is living an unbalanced life. Few people live more unbalanced lives than business owners.

A business can be a jealous mistress and its demands can crowd out other parts of life. When the business is gone it leaves a void, an emptiness, that, if not filled by other things, can lead to depression. And as if running a business isn't demanding enough, layering the demands of a business sale on top further crowds out friends, family, and other activities, making the void that much larger when the transaction is complete and the owner walks away.

"I fell into a funk," admitted one. "Well, maybe funk is not the right word. I was depressed. I still got up early every morning, but there wasn't a reason to. I'd check email and there wasn't anything worth reading. It was like I ceased to exist."

"You would think I'd be on top of the world," said another former owner. "I'd just fulfilled the dream. I had generational wealth. I had everything. And yet, if felt like I had nothing. I'm not alone. There's a guy in my industry who hit it big time, like hundreds of millions of dollars big time. He told me that he went through a bout of depression following the sale of his business."

Like the reluctance to admit to burnout before the sale, few business owners would admit to feeling depressed afterward. Still, they confessed the symptoms of depression. "Maybe not right away, but I think after about a month or two after I left is when I started really thinking about things. I said it to my wife. I think that the biggest thing is I've lost a lot of stuff. I lost power. I lost going to the office and just being around other people. So, that's been a big change, going from doing things all your life and then coming home and just having that in place."

Depression isn't limited to the former owner. One described watching one of his key people become depressed after the business sold. "He was very negative. Just a very unhappy, negative guy. He's always the life-of-the-party guy, and it changed his personality to the point that he was not fun to be around. It wasn't just me. We have similar friends and they're asking what the hell's wrong with him? I tried initially to help him mentally come around, and then I realized that nothing I was saying was going to help. I was kind of counseling him. Dude, you need to just move on."

Type-A personalities seem more prone to depression than others. These are people who are used to a go-go approach and have trouble when there's nothing left to drive toward. They can be business-adrenaline junkies who go through withdrawal upon walking away.

Some business owners, particularly type-A personalities, may face depression after walking away. Business owners should prepare for it and the need to work through it.

59. Remorse

Former owners frequently experience some level of seller's remorse even when they're generally pleased with the sale. "I looked in the mirror and asked myself, *Do I want to do it again?* I have a friend over in Austin who needs help. I am going to help him with some things. But it's like I do not want to start thinking about doing a business again. I just don't feel like getting back involved in the whole thing. I do go back and forth on this, but I defiantly one hundred percent do not regret selling. Everything went great, so there definitely isn't any regret."

"There's some regrets associated with selling the business," said another. "If I had stayed with the business, what's not to say that everybody wouldn't have still been taken care of? There's a pretty good chance that the business still would have succeeded. I would have continued working for several more years. My wife and I would still be set. The employees would be taken care of. Obviously, we should still be able to take care of the kids and grandkids. The difference is that is you think and hope that it's going to happen. Now we know we can. So that's probably the one regret, missing out on running the business."

"I think it was an ultimate success for me personally because I've got the money in the bank," admitted another former owner. "Do I have regrets? Yeah, I would do things a little differently, but as far as the company, I think it was successful."

"I had a company I bought, and a year later we had doubled the business, tripled the EBITDA," noted a buyer. "They were sitting there saying, 'Damn, I shouldn't have sold it!' But of course, they likely wouldn't have grown it by themselves."

"A buddy of mine was talking about how they're building their company for the family and the next generation," said a former owner. "The next generation. And family is the most important thing and this and that. When I hear stuff like that, I think I sold out. I sold out on my boys. But assuming the next turn [or sale], turns out the way it's supposed to, my kids will benefit. They already have, but they'll get real benefit someday. It probably won't take me dying for that to happen. We'll build something before that. But sometimes there's regret there or perceived regret."

He continued, "My two oldest boys are doing great. My youngest has only been in the workforce for about 18 months. He actually started a month before we sold. He was the one that I think really thought he had an opportunity to come help run it or take it over. I think the older boys figured out that they weren't going to be there. It is tough. When I talked to my youngest son a couple of months ago and he said it was different than all the other jobs he ever had because he had this pride of ownership, even though he was just a kid. That made me regret it too. That hurt."

"Have you ever seen, a grown man cry?" asked another former owner. "My wife didn't see it. I cried all the way home. It was pretty horrifying. I thought, *Oh, God, what do I do now?*"

For every business owner who felt seller's remorse, there's another who had zero remorse. One said, "I do not regret selling at all. I see the new guy with the challenges. He comes to me and asks me questions about how to handle this and that, so I am certainly still in the fold as somewhat of an advisor. I get my fill as an advisor, but if we scratch someone's hardwood floors, it is not my problem anymore."

One former owner said, "I don't think I'd do anything different. I can't think of anything. I really can't."

Another said, "I have no regrets. None. Zero. Nada. I feel good about it. It worked out well. I keep in touch with a handful of employees. They still call me and ask for advice every now and then. And I miss some of those relationships. But aside from that, whenever I start feeling that sense of remorse, or missing something, I have to remind myself I'm remembering the good parts and I need to also remember the bad."

A business owner's perspective on the business can make a huge difference. One said, "I made a conscious decision that it's my family's wealth. It's not a business. It's not an enterprise. It's not anything but my family's wealth, long-term. And once you go in with that attitude, it makes a difference. It all depends on where you look at it from. Why am I here? I'm here to take care of my family. How do I take care of my family? It's not about the accomplishment. It's about 100 years from now. What's going to matter is how my grandkids and their kids are."

Seller's remorse tends to fade over time. One owner noted that it took a year and a half to get past it. He said, "I had regrets for the first 18 months. Yes. I would regret it. Every minute of it, for the first

18 months. I was so sorry. I've been in that business my whole life from the time I was 13 years old until present."

Sometimes the remorse is compartmentalized. For example, a former owner expressed remorse that he could no longer support the same local charities through the business. He said, "The tough thing is all the nonprofits that I've supported and all the friends and family that still think I own the business. The new owner may not care about the same nonprofits I do. When some of those people come calling that you've been dealing with for 30-plus years and you have to say no because that's not the motivation of the owner. That's tough. Now, can I do that stuff personally? Absolutely. Quite often, what I do is just put the elements coming from the company and write the personal check and have them use the company logo. But those are the tougher things that are probably going to get tougher, more in the future than they are now."

Another expressed the remorse that a parent might express when watching a child grow up and begin to develop his own life. He said, "It wasn't just a company. It was people. It was a team that was growing and evolving and maturing together. And I got to watch that. It was a little bit like this kid who's ready for middle school and I've got to just let it go."

This former owner, happy with the direction the company took after he gave up control, felt pride and a measure of joy watching it continue. "Today, growth is still happening in that company. And I'm so proud of the team down there and what I developed now, with it being in the rearview mirror. It's been several years. There's still twinges of pain, but the burst of joy that I get when I see them online makes me very proud and happy. I was able to help build a company that is now a full-grown adult, caring for itself. The people are well cared for. The product is exceptional. They have a whole team of people that are working very well together. To see that go from zero to where it is today, even though the sale was extremely painful... I feel like I was able to help them set a foundation culturally and set some fiscal guardrails to keep strong financially, and then to develop a team of people and develop themselves. Even though I just occasionally get to see this young son of mine, I'll refer to it as that, it just makes me burst with pride. This is something that, without me, and without God, never would have happened."

For this former owner, business is a mission. He concluded, "They take 10% of their net income and they give it away. They take their team members on mission trips. They build things for missionaries. They're involved in the community. It's just a real testament of what can happen when you do things the right way. And for me, that's doing things God's way. I give God the glory because He's the one who ultimately put it together and did it, and I just got to be a small part of it."

Another former owner said, "For the company itself, it was not a successful undertaking. I think it was an ultimate success for me personally because I got the money in the bank. Do I have regrets? Yeah, I would do things a little differently, but I think it was that successful."

No matter how many regrets were expressed, there wasn't a single business owner interviewed who regretted taking the money from the sale of the business. Not a single one would give the money back in exchange for the business. Admittedly, one buyer did report on unwinding a sale from a regretful owner during the days immediately following the close, but that single example is the only one encountered.

Business owners may have second thoughts about selling, but not enough to give the money back. Thus, business owners should brush off seller's remorse.

60: Post-Sale Conflict

Conflicts over money can occur after the sale. This is one of the reasons business owners should be satisfied with the money received at close. Fortunately, most conflicts get resolved without litigation, but not always.

A buyer explained how he tried to address conflicts. "If there is controversy, then we can bring in someone to arbitrate. We try to cover those bases up front."

One business owner got into a dispute with the buyer over work-in-progress. Contractually, the seller was owed the money. The buyer was delaying payments, in all likelihood due to cash flow. A major account had stopped ordering. "It wasn't even that the business relationship had changed," noted the seller. "They just didn't have any more business for him. There was no contract guaranteeing any amount of business. And the final sale agreement said that we don't make any guarantees of future business. When I sent my legal letter stating that I need to get paid on the work-in-progress, he responded with a claim of fraud against me, saying that I knew the major account was going to go on a hiatus before the sale, that I went through the sale without disclosing that, therefore, I've committed fraud, and he wants more than 15 times my demand-for-payment that he contractually agreed to pay. That's where the emotions really hit."

The former owner continued, "Gosh dang it. I don't want to get into a two-year lawsuit. I was done with this. I had done a good job, but I felt kind of like a failure. How did I screw this up? How could I have prevented this from happening? I was scared because I've worked my ass off and he's going to come after my family now. I felt like I put my family at risk by putting us in the situation even though I didn't do anything wrong. I had this fear and this question of my integrity. I just had disgust for him. How could this guy do it? And eventually I started to think he planned this all along."

She continued, "On top of everything else, he had my employees writing statements against me saying that I knew that this was going to happen. I took care of these people. I made so many sacrifices for these people. They were willing to throw me to the fire as soon as the new guy stepped in. It's, 'Okay, who's paying my paycheck now? Okay, I'll go with whatever he says.' I understand why they did it. I just think they're pieces of crap for doing it."

The former owner chose mediation, which ultimately failed, and she came to realize the buyer simply didn't have the money to pay the work-in-progress and would declare bankruptcy. This also meant the buyer lacked the resources to fund litigation for his claims. Finally, the former owner just walked away, saying, "It's been a really hard lesson, but I've found peace in giving it to God and letting Him take it where it needs to go."

When conflicts emerge, they're often centered on earn-outs. When the former owner fails to achieve an earn-out he starts looking for things the buyer did that might have impeded him. This includes overhead that was assigned to his P&L, control over marketing, and so on. While earn-outs can be incredibly positive, they can create conflict, resulting in a me-versus-them attitude on the part of the former owner.

Another conflict that was reported involved a tax issue that emerged after the holdback was returned. The former owner said, "It was an issue that came up as part of the ownership change. I wanted to hire a local tax consultant who deals with these all of the time. He would have cost $1,500 and saved us five figures. Corporate's controller disagreed and literally ordered me not to hire the consultant. So I asked him what he proposed doing and he said he'd just pay it. I thought, *It's your money. What the hell?* Part of the dispute stretched back to my time as owner and the controller told me I was liable for it. I said, 'No. You're too late. The holdback's been returned and distributed.' He said it doesn't matter for tax issues. I refused to pay it and it went back and forth for years with the corporate attorney getting involved and sending me nasty emails. Finally, I went over the lawyer's head to the CEO and he backed me, so it all worked out."

While rare, some transactions go sideways and result in conflict. Business owners should be careful to tamp down the emotion and cut losses to avoid situations where only the lawyers win.

61: Staying Busy

Owning a business is an active job. There's always something going on, some hill to climb, some crisis to solve, some urgent matter demanding immediate attention. Staying busy is the last problem most business owners have... until they sell. Many recognize the importance of staying busy when they aren't working. Some take on odd jobs around their house or a second property. Some work on their health and fitness. Some find new careers, including new businesses or investments. Some immerse themselves in volunteer work.

"My plan," declared a former owner, "was to definitely stay physically active. I go to the gym with a trainer Tuesday and Thursday, which I've always done, but then I got a bike. I bike Monday through Wednesday. We just finished a 54-mile bike race a month ago. I'm a horrible, horrible swimmer. So, I've been taking swim lessons. They start up again in May."

A former owner immersed herself in volunteer work. She said, "The work that I'm doing now I really enjoy. I can go back to being 18 years old and participating in Special Olympics to help out. I love the connection of the people. Saturday, I'm going to do a talk up in our little town for different scholarships and things like that. That's where my identity is. It's in helping, serving, working with the people. And I love all this mentoring. I mentor a lot of people. That's what fills me up. I enjoy that stuff. We do Habitat builds. We do things like that."

Yet another recognized the need to be busy. She said, "I asked myself, what am I going to do? I can't sit around. I want to keep my brain sharp, and I have so much I could share."

A friend told her, "You need to take at least six months off for you. Say yes to nothing. You do nothing but relax, travel, enjoy, eat, travel, sleep, whatever you want to do. Ideally, it'd be 365 days. Ideally, it's a year, but most people can't last a year, but take at least six months." She did. "For the first three months, I literally did nothing. I was so tired. I went to India with my husband. We traveled. I exercised, organized my house, all that kind of stuff."

Another former owner noted, "You've got to stay active. You've got to come up with something that you have passion about and whatever that is."

Jacob and Michel

Some business owners are only wired for business. Business is their hobby. It's what they enjoy doing. They aren't going to restore classic cars. They aren't going to volunteer for their Rotary Clubs. They're going to start another business. Their challenge is finding one that's interesting to them and doesn't violate their non-compete.

"I started buying real estate," noted one. "While I was traveling, I was buying. I bought a little two-bedroom house, turned it into my office, hired an accountant to run my real estate business, and put him in the office there so he could take care of things while I was gone. I started buying small houses within a mile. I wanted to be able to walk to any one of our properties and put the accountant in charge of finding them. We picked up the average property for about 140,000 dollars and would rent them out for 1400 dollars a month. I think we had 27 homes at peak after three years. I did all that while I was traveling."

A former owner who could only imagine starting another business said, "We're thinking about doing a handyman service, then use those proceeds to start the other locations." While he didn't ultimately start the handyman service, he did open a garage door company.

Business ownership involves lots of activity. Former owners should prepare for something to fill the void after walking away from their companies.

62: Income Streams

Men, it seems, are happier with life if they have an income stream arising from their efforts, separate from any investment income. Women don't appear to share this characteristic. Presumably, this is the result of men tending to derive a good part of their self-worth based on their incomes.

"I still have a scarcity mentality," confessed a former owner who sold his company for a healthy amount. "I need a paycheck."

There is a fear of running out of money. Multi-millionaire sellers may be set for life, but they cannot escape a nagging feeling that somehow, some way, their assets might evaporate or devalue so that they run out of money. An income stream seems to help offset this fear.

A former owner, who didn't need to work after selling his company, said, "If I didn't have an income coming in I would probably have some financial regrets. My son and I were talking about that. It makes a whole big difference. It comes in every week, not just once a month. If I didn't have that, I would be a lot more antsy and maybe want to work. If I didn't have that income, then that would be a game changer."

Another said, "It was ridiculous. I was chasing consulting gigs that wouldn't violate my non-compete. I did freelance work and even thought about Fiverr. I pondered going to work for a couple of people. Finally, my financial advisor kind of mentally slapped me. My passive income from investments was seven figures a year. My lifestyle was a fraction of that. And here I was chasing my tail trying to scratch out extra income just because that's what I'd done my whole life. Since my first job, I'd never been without a paycheck. It was extremely uncomfortable to be without one, even though I didn't need it."

A good financial advisor can help wealthy business owners overcome an irrational fear of scarcity. "We went to see our financial advisor for a review of our situation. I was terrified going into the meeting. I thought he was going to tell us we needed to stop spending money. We were spending about a million dollars a year while our investments were increasing around two million a year. Granted, the markets have been good and won't always be this good. The financial advisor helped me wrap my head around the fact that we were okay and would be okay."

Men, in particular, seem to need an income stream, resulting from their direct effort, to maintain their sense of self-worth. Male business owners should consider a small hobby business or other income-producing activity.

63: Former Employees

Most sellers have few expectations of their former employees. Others exhibit a paternalistic attitude. They feel that they've taken care of them and sacrificed for them through the years and are surprised and disappointed when the employees fail to display the gratitude they feel is their due.

One former owner, who had few expectations, admitted that he played somewhat of a paternalistic role that continued after the business was sold. He said, "They send me pictures of their kids playing, their softball team or baseball team, or whatever. I'm the grandpa. They're all younger."

Relationships with former employees can be complicated. Some will be personally loyal, but most immediately transfer their fealty to the people who sign their paychecks. One former owner confessed, "The only thing that was a big, big, big surprise for me was my employees. I went to such great effort to take care of my employees for the whole time they worked for me. I was so kind to people after they left. I cannot even count on one hand, well, less than five fingers, how many people have reached out to me."

She noted that, "One employee reached out to me and said, 'I am so grateful for the opportunity you gave me. I would love to take you to lunch.' She's the only person."

"A lot of my employees were probably worried about their jobs more than anything," said another former owner. "You would be, too, if it was your paycheck. When they heard that it was a larger company that had years and years of experience and some real good people, there were questions. Nobody quit until after I left. Then it was like rats overboard when they found out that the company was changing things up. There were no hard feelings towards me. I have my employees, my key employees, over to the ranch twice a year, and we just have a blast. They're good people, but every one of them made out just fine."

Because relationships extend for years and even decades, there is a desire on the part of former owners to maintain the relationships. While this seems fine on the surface, it can adversely impact employee attitudes towards the new owners. The healthiest relationships seem be the ones where the former owner remains passive. He listens, but refrains from offering his opinion, which isn't always easy.

Jacob and Michel

"Once I left," noted a former owner, "I never dropped by the office. I never called unless it was something specific, like COBRA [health insurance]. But I did take calls. I did accept lunch invitations. I listened to what people told me and did my best not to comment. About all I said when someone griped was, 'It's their company.'"

Another commented, "I still hear from a lot of those employees and everything else. It was different when I sold. I still keep my same phone number. I still have employees who will call me for one reason or another. It's people you'd never think would call you. Even now, today, I'll get a call every once in a while, people asking for some advice or whatever the case may be."

"Do you remember the movie *St. Elmo's Fire?*" asked a former owner. "In the movie, there's this guy who was the fraternity stud while he was in college. He never got over that period in his life and goes back to the old fraternity. Everyone's glad to see him. He's a legend. But he wants to stay. He wants to be part of it. One of the guys tells him he can't. He's graduated. He needs to move on. Well, that's kind of what it's like when you sell your company and leave. You remember it like a fraternity, but you're not an active member anymore. The guys still there like you, but you're not a part of it any longer. There's no place for you. If you haven't found something to replace it, it can be hard to take."

Employees will gripe about the new owners. In fact, many seem to think their old bosses would rather hear how the new owners are screwing up than how they are making improvements. Some employees simply resist change, and with new ownership there will be changes. Some will be good. Some will be bad. Most will simply be different.

When a former owner injects an adverse opinion about decisions made by the new owners he harms his team and stirs dissent. He lets his ego get ahead of his checking account. When he accepted payment, he gave up the right to comment.

Former owners should be careful when discussing the company with their former employees. By accepting payment, the owner cedes the right to comment.

64: Travel

A small but significant number of former owners elect to travel internationally after walking away from their companies. They feel they couldn't take the time for long excursions when operating their companies. After leaving, not only do they have the time, they have the financial resources. One said, "We had a lot of plans. We had a getaway to Kauai for two weeks. There was a lot of things to do. We haven't had a vacation. When's the last time we had a frigging vacation? Never. Two weeks. Yeah. So we had some distractions right away, and we were celebrating 50 years being married. So that was a wonderful thing."

"I traveled the world for three years," said another. "I went to every place I'd ever dreamed of going to. I've been to all seven continents and some 70 countries, from Mount Everest to Antarctica. I just waited until the business was sold and said, okay, the first place is I want to be in a picture of me on the beach with that penguin in the Antarctic. So I got on a ship with a bunch of scientists and spent ten days there."

Another, who developed a measured pace of travel, said, "I go out of the country once a year. I like to. We're leaving in June for France, Germany, the Netherlands and Switzerland. My sister-in-law gave me this book. It's the national parks of the U.S., so we try to visit one a quarter or something like that. I have a childhood friend from fourth grade and we still think we're young men. We went hiking in Big Bend and realized we're not that young anymore."

Yet another simply enjoyed not only the means, but the personal freedom to be able to travel. "I really enjoyed getting to be able to travel freely. If we want to go to Europe, we went to Europe, that kind of stuff."

Several reported spending a lot of time hunting and fishing. One said, "I love Amelia Island, Florida, because the tarpon fishing is great there. I was in Big Sky, Montana, last August. I caught a ton of trout. I've been to Alaska, halibut fishing. That's great... We go down to the coast a couple times a year. I'm going in May. I've been to Cabo and Hawaii. Hawaii wasn't that great. Venice, Louisiana, is really good. I went down to Belize and did some bone fishing, and that was good."

"I had a plan," noted another former owner. "I was going to make up for all of the missed hunting and fishing trips through the years. I planned a hunting or fishing trip every month for the first two years. These weren't small trips. Well, some of them were. A lot of them were 'travel the world' trips for trophy fish and game. It was fun. It wasn't enough. I need a greater purpose in life than hunting and fishing."

This is a typical response from those who travel. The journeys may last as long as three years, but when they end, or when they run out of places they want to see, they're faced with the same challenges most former owners deal with: What do I do next?

The travel, while rewarding, merely delays the day of reckoning. They must still figure out what they want to do with their lives.

Many former owners, especially those who felt chained to their companies, embrace travel after selling. If desired, they should take advantage of their newfound freedom and wealth to travel the world.

65: Buyer Mistakes

A common complaint of former owners is that the buyers wrecked their companies. Certainly, the landscape is littered with the remains of broken companies that didn't long survive their founders' departures, but the reality isn't always so dire. Since former owners are hypercritical of buyer stewardship, their perspective tends to be skewed.

An investment banker said, "Former business owners who cry about what the buyer is doing to 'my business' are common. But in reality, their businesses are no longer theirs and are now owned by the buyers. They would save themselves a lot of unnecessary stress and grief if they accepted that before going into the sale. They need to tell themselves, 'If the check clears, it's no longer mine.' Get over it. Go see the world. Take your wife on vacation. Life is short and you now have financial freedom. If the buyer changes the look of your logo or terminates your assistant controller, so be it."

Nevertheless, it seems complaining about the new owners is a more popular sport than golf. One owner said about his former partner, "We can't spend a couple hours together without him complaining about the private equity firm is taking his marketing and totally screwing it up."

Yet the pain that some experience, helplessly watching the businesses they built get slowly torn apart, is real. One said, "As months go on, the employees were unhappy and I felt that pain. It was really hard emotionally. To be honest, that was the most painful part of it. I knew to expect it. People told me it would happen, but it's not the same as experiencing it and seeing your baby get slaughtered and butchered with all the stupid-ass decisions. We had a great name in the marketplace. Corporate with their big ego wanted to immediately rebrand. It could have been a transition over a period of time so the book of business doesn't evaporate. They didn't do that. There was a lot of pain and I felt it. There was nothing I could do about it."

Complaints about changing the branding are common. "They got a little slap happy with the brand and wanting to rebrand everything, a new logo, a new font. I told him, 'Dude, there's so many bigger things to focus on than rebranding.' I worked in marketing communications for more than 20 years. The buyer didn't want to hear my opinion on logo design. I told him, 'Dude, I ran a marketing department for a multi-million-dollar education company. I've written marketing materials for… I can't tell you how many businesses and across multiple industries, everything from literally pet food to oil and gas to senior living. I know me some marketing.' They didn't want my input on the logo."

Usually, buyers make changes gradually. In some cases, they're too busy buying companies to focus on the companies they already bought. In other cases, they study the acquisitions and wait until they believe they know where improvements are needed. One former owner talked about the timing. He said, "For the first year they didn't make any changes. I found out that private equity is not as organized as the corporations. Things fall through the cracks. Communication is really bad. At first, everything ran as normal and then it happened, like in the second year. You go into the third year, that's when I think they really looked at the numbers and they said, 'Hey, wait a second. We're not being as profitable as we thought we would be. So we're going to start cutting everything back.'"

Former owners should accept that what happens with their old businesses isn't their responsibility. It belongs to the buyer, and the business owner was duly compensated. When former owners lament the changes buyers make, all they accomplish is making themselves miserable. One confessed, "I kept a running log of all of the stupid moves the new owners made. After a couple of years, it finally sunk in that this was pointless and all I was doing was frustrating myself. I couldn't do anything about it. Look, selling was the right thing to do and while I let go legally, I hadn't let go emotionally. So one day I just kind of let go all the way. I could count my money and be happy or count the things they did that pissed me off and be unhappy."

Sometimes, buyers do not want to make changes, even if the business environment is changing. Another former owner said, "My role, when it was my company, was to look around the corner. What's going to be the next thing that happens in our industry? What vendors do we need to associate with? What services and products do we need to be selling? And I was trying to do that same role within the new company. Their attitude was, 'Hey, we got something that's working. We're not going to jack with it.' Well, you can't really do that with technology."

Business owners who are well compensated need to let go of their old businesses and embrace a new business: the business of managing their portfolios.

The Business-Exit Roller Coaster

Some buyers will wreck the businesses they acquire, at least in the seller's view. Business owners need to remember, they are NOT their businesses.

Jacob and Michel

66: Wealth

In his book *Strangers in Paradise: How Families Adapt to Wealth Across Generations,* Dr. James Grubman describes how the onset of wealth is like moving to another country. There are new rules and responsibilities. It's easy to feel isolated. Grubman writes, "Family and friends back home will not know how to handle the change in relationships."

New wealth does impact people. Some deny the impact and refuse to change how they live. They don't allow themselves to enjoy the money that hard work, good decision-making, and smart risk-taking blessed them with.

Others go a little crazy and may even blow their bounty. They make lavish purchases. They make poor investments.

"I talked to a friend who sold his company when [the private equity wave] first started," said a former owner. "He asked me, 'Will this money change your life? It changed *my* life.' No, it won't. It'll make me financially set, where I wouldn't have to work. I could walk away and make six figures a year for the rest of my life. I'd have to live a — not an extravagant lifestyle, but it wouldn't change my life because life's more than money and money's not my driving goal. It never has been. But the day of transaction, knowing that there's multi-millions of dollars in my account and I am financially set... it was amazing. And it was a very, very humbling, very emotional time. It was just... It was just mind-blowing that this high-school kid who only had the ambition when he got out of school to get a job, to make enough money to buy beer, was now in the top 1% of wealth earners in this country!"

The trick business owners strive for is a middle ground where they feel comfortable enjoying their wealth and using it to do good for others. For most, spending money does not come easily. It's counter to a lifetime of careful management of their financials and their businesses. "When I first sold the company, I did the math all the time," said a former owner. "I would figure out my liquid net worth and divide it by 30 more years or 35 more years. What I didn't realize, and probably should have, is that it's an entity that generates its own wealth, too. It generates its own income." In other words, invested wealth is not static. It generates income and grows on its own as long as spending remains below the investment return."

"Money to me is a necessary evil," said another. "My wife and I live on a budget. We limit what we do. I limit myself on purpose because money is one of two things to me. It's either going to be my friend or it's going to be a serpent that will take me out. And I've seen that happen to so many guys. And so that's why we live on a budget. I could live in a mansion of a house. We live in a nice house. It's definitely not a mansion, but it's very nice. We travel, we do things, but we absolutely live on a budget. It's because I grew up with absolutely nothing. I grew up hungry, cold, and in violence, lived in a violent home. My father was an abusive alcoholic. I dropped out of school, high school, and in the 10th grade, midway through the 10th grade, I went to work."

"Everybody wanted to prepare me for some giant change in my life," said another former owner. "It's all going to be different and all these things, but I had enough friends who had already sold their companies for a million here and a million there. Only one sold for like 50 million. That changed his life. But my company didn't sell for that much money and the lifestyle change was not drastic. I just had less stress and worry."

One former owner commented, "I have a wealthy friend who sits on a board with me. After I sold the company, he began prodding me to let go of some of it and use it for my enjoyment and my family's enjoyment. It was hard for me. It's still hard. I still look for discounts and sales. I hesitate to drive in the toll lanes. I fly in coach. I can't help it. It's how I'm wired. You know what he said? He said, 'If you won't fly first class, your kids will.'"

Another former owner said, "I keep telling entrepreneurs who cashed out to spend your money. You can't squeeze one penny into the coffin."

"We were doing financial models with my financial guy," said another, "and he said, 'When are you going to start living? You're 62. You can't play golf at a high level past 75 maybe. You can't do a lot after that."

As former owners age, attitudes toward their wealth can change. One said, "I got more money than I can ever spend, guarantee you. We try to spend money, and we really can't. We can't even spend enough to stop the interest on what we're making off the money. I tell my wife, 'We're rich. Go ahead and buy it.' But remember, that's something new to us. For years, we said, 'No, save the money.' But today, because I've got a lot of money, I give a lot of money away.

Jacob and Michel

I've given over a million bucks to my alma mater. I think I'm up to 1.2 million dollars."

Many business owners who become wealthy through the sale of their companies become very intentional about giving some away. "My wife and I have a trust," said one. "We channel a lot of money through a trust, and there's a board of directors that gives the money away."

Another commented, "I used to fantasize about money. I remember there was a commercial on TV about some investment company. They had a guy all dressed up nice, and he had his horse with him, and he's walking down a trail, and the trail comes to his house, which is not his house, it's his mailbox. And you can see this long path to his house, okay? He opens up the mailbox, takes the mail out and opens it up, which became his investment portfolio information for the month. He unfolds it and he smiles. And I thought, you lucky SOB! How can that be? Well, I have that now. I've got more money than I can spend."

Just as former owners who hired experts to represent them did better through the sales process, those who hired a good financial advisor or fiduciary to help them manage their portfolio did better with their gains. A good financial advisor will put together a plan to protect wealth, consistent with the risk tolerance of the former business owner, while continuing to grow it.

One seller got a surprise call from his banker after his transaction funded. He said, "It wasn't like the wire was giant. It was a couple million. The banker asked, 'Is there something we need to talk about?' I said, 'No, no, I just sold a business.' He said, 'Well, we have these wealth management people. We need for you to talk to us.'"

"I thought money was just something sitting there," said another. "It was a big pile of gold and you took money off the pile when you needed it. In 2008, I was invested almost 100% in large-cap stocks, which were the first to go. I almost halved my portfolio. The good news is I had enough. I said, 'Don't pull it out, because then you pay taxes.' I left it all alone. I left it totally intact. A lot of guys will tell you about this stock deal they did and how much money they made. And what they don't tell you is all the times they screwed up. By 2011, my stock portfolio was back where I had it. And then I got rid of the stock. I said, 'No more of this.' I got into a lot of bonds. Bonds are wonderful.

"Now I think of money as something that's extremely hard to take care of. It's not something you just let sit there and look at. Well, should I move this to that? How much tax-exempt municipal bonds should I have? I've got a Merrill Lynch guy that I've known for 20 years, and he calls me every now and then. 'Well, let's move this to that and that to these.' And it's interesting to me because it just keeps going up. I can't make it go down. I've done well. I'm happy. If I die tomorrow, I'm happy."

No doubt there are people in every business owner's network who can recommend a trustworthy financial advisor or wealth management advisor. Nevertheless, some former owners try to manage their wealth on their own by day trading and other ventures. With day trading, they pay short-term capital gains for most trades and are less likely to take advantage of tax-harvesting strategies. They also seem more likely to invest in cryptocurrencies and gold rather than stocks and bonds as an inflation hedge.

"I'm not day trading," declared a former owner. "I'm not doing anything like that. I've got money with Merrill Lynch and I've got money with Goldman Sachs and the S&P 500. It doubles every nine, ten years. I'm going to see how many doubling cycles I can do. I'm not trying to be a hero. I'm not trying to outsmart the market or time the market. I'm going to work. My wife's an attorney. She owns her own law firm, so she's done very well for herself. So we plan on living off our Social Security, our IRAs, our retirements, and our 401(k)s. We plan on never touching the nest egg."

A buyer said, "I think if someone is thinking about selling their business, they need to understand what their next steps are. So you don't just go sell. What are you planning to do afterwards? Are you planning to start a different company? Are you planning to just sell and no longer be in this industry? I think that makes all the difference in the world if you're just going to sell and ride off into the sunset, have a good life, rest, relax. Make sure you have plenty of money, make sure you have some stream of income coming in, those type of things."

He continued, cautioning against starting a new business in an unrelated field. He said, "If you're just getting ready to sell and you want to start a new venture, really do your diligence and understand what you're getting into. What I have seen over the years is people who have money, who acquire money all of a sudden, want to start all these different things. Maybe I'll open up a coffee shop. Maybe I'll go do this and do that. Unless you're locked and loaded, chances are you're going to have a hard time making it. Your money at some point is not going to overcome those challenges."

A few former owners noted that they were treated differently by people after they sold their companies. One said, "It was odd at first.

It was like people listened to me more. There was a deference that I'd never felt. Maybe it's just me and maybe I'm paranoid, but I'm a little more wary of people now."

When pressed to elaborate, he added, "When someone didn't seem too interested in associating with you suddenly changes and the change coincides with a financial windfall, you start to wonder. Some of it is so subtle… it's just hard to explain. But it's there."

Another was more explicit. "People look at you like, you're a rich guy, man. You're loaded. You don't even have to work. And so people treat you differently. And it's not a good feeling for a personality type like mine, because I take it all personal. It hurt when I sensed that people looked at me differently because I didn't have to work. I've got the same friends I've always had. They're not wealthy people and their day-to-day worries are not the things that I worry about. We still have a relationship, but it's different now."

Adjusting to wealth is a challenge. Professional financial advice can help former owners enjoy their wealth and use it for causes important to them.

67: Estate Planning

In addition to a financial advisor, many business owners seek an attorney who specializes in family law and estate planning. Trusts are set up to maximize the inheritance of heirs and to protect assets from litigation and from the spouses of children if a marriage fails. "Our financial advisor recommended an estate attorney," said a former owner. "The attorney set up our entire estate plan, including an LLC and trusts for my wife and me and for our kids whenever we pass. It's complex, but probably boilerplate for the attorney. Anyway, the plan didn't cost a lot and it protects us and our kids."

Another noted, "I spent a lot of time with the wealth management guy so that I could make sure that whatever I got, the money would work for me."

"If something happens to me," explained another, "we have a trigger that everything immediately transfers to our trust and a board of men that will handle it and make sure that our wishes are going to be carried out and that the funds through the sales of these companies are going to go into the right hands. My wife and I have eight children. We've already given them their inheritance, so they know that when we die, there's not going to be any fighting."

Estate planning becomes more important when wealth grows beyond the tax-free limits of inheritance, which is subject to change when the political winds shift. Without proper planning, the government can seize a significant share of an entrepreneur's estate.

Tax avoidance is only part of the story. This is the arena of generational wealth, which has the potential to change the lives of children, grandchildren, and future generations. It can also destroy lives.

William K. Vanderbilt, the grandson of Cornelius Vanderbilt, one of the richest men in the history of the United States, claimed, "Inherited wealth is a real handicap to happiness. It is as certain a death to ambition as cocaine is to morality."

"Shirtsleeves to shirtsleeves in three generations" is more than an adage; it's all too true. Some business owners fear the loss of the wealth they've built and create a process for embedding a culture in their families that's similar to what they did for their companies, with the hope that culture will guide the family long after the owner has passed away.

"We've set up some generation-skipping trusts just to prevent shirtsleeves to shirtsleeves," a business owner said. "We're making it kind of flexible on what they get. If my wife and I live on what we've allotted and budgeted, when we pass, we'll have more than we started with, without exception. So now, what do we do with that to make sure it doesn't get squandered? It's just trying to set it up so that it can't be abused."

He continued, "We're with a fiduciary. They don't even get any commissions from trades or whatever. It's all part of the fees. They make a percent on the invested value of the assets under management and they'll do everything for us. If I got to set up a wire transfer to buy a truck, I call them and say, 'Can you set this up?' 'Sure. Just let us know when to send it.' For some older trusts they pay all the monthly bills. They are full-service wealth management if you need it. They don't advertise it, but if you need it, they'll do it for you. And to that point, I don't have to worry about it."

A serial entrepreneur said, "I chose to form a 501(c)(3) and have this foundation set up to handle my estate. Even before I'm dead and gone, it will start to manage some of these profit centers and some of these companies."

"I've got a couple boys that are just getting out of college," said another former owner. "This impacts them potentially way more than me. I've got maybe 30 years to deal with. What do I do with this money? And they potentially have, Lord willing, 80 years to deal with it. That's a big deal."

Another talked about trusts and real estate investments. "I'm a real estate guy. Real estate is going to have its ups and downs, but it's never going to be worth zero. I'm creating a trust where my family has a role, where there are going to be properties that may need to be sold for different reasons. Either it's a tax issue because we're making too much money, or it's falling apart. But I'm setting it up where the money from any sale can only be reinvested back into the trust, back into more real estate. We're allowing the heirs to take 50 or 60% of the proceeds, free and clear, the rest of those going back into more investment."

Another, thinking about future generations, said, "We've got three girls and we've got three weddings to pay for. We plan on looking forward to the grandparent job. That looks like the coolest thing I've seen anybody do, being a grandparent and helping them with down payments on their houses and stuff like that."

"When I sold," a former owner said, "I told the wealth management guy to make sure I always have money every year to pay to take the entire family, everybody, and their families, to go on vacation. I have certain charities, the food bank, St. Jude, and others. So I created a charitable trust."

Money can make life easier, but it can also ruin people who aren't prepared for it. Business owners with generational wealth should seek legal and wealth management advice to ensure their assets are protected and that future generations will benefit.

Jacob and Michel

68: Relationships

Entrepreneurs often don't understand how relationships tend to end when business transactions cease. There may be friendships, but the anchor is the business relationship. Once the business owner sells his company, he's not going to be going on European incentive trips with his old buddies. His oil-field equipment supplier isn't going to invite him to the weekly crawfish boil. There are no tickets to football games, no invitations to pheasant hunts, and no more connections to those people. It's not that the relationships were superficial, they were just cemented by a business relationship that no longer exists.

The business is the intersection of these relationships. Once they walk away from their companies, business owners may realize they're walking away from a significant number of relationships. Absent the business, they simply don't encounter the same people without intentional effort.

"The first time I missed the big industry trade show was hard," said one former owner. "It was harder because of social media. I'm watching all of these people post on LinkedIn and Facebook and it was killing me not to be there. Yet there wasn't any reason for me to be at the show. I thought of the people I know who retired in the past and didn't really remember any interactions. It was almost like they died. So is that me now?"

Some former owners continue to attend industry shows just to maintain connections. One remarked, "I used to think it was kind of pathetic when someone who retired or sold his business continued to show up at a trade show. Now I'm doing it. I'm just not ready to close that chapter of my life, and if I'm going to start a new business in a couple of years, I need to keep in touch with people."

Another former owner said, "One of the worst things was not being around the people like I was. I still engage with them. I still go out to lunch with them and things like that. I'm still keeping a connection. But it's not the same."

There does appear to be a difference in attitudes about relationships. Former owners who ran locally focused companies were more blasé about the potential loss of relationships. "The people I worked with are all located around here," said the seller of a locally focused business. "We can go to lunch anytime we want." When asked if he had done that with any of them, he said he hadn't. But the fact that he easily could seemed to make a difference.

One former owner explained how a past experience prepared him for a loss of relationships. "I was the president of our national trade association, so I traveled 169 days. I was part of their executive board for five years. And the day you're not past president anymore, you don't get an email. You don't. You know it's coming. It's nothing you're even upset about, but it's hard. You can reach out and call somebody or email people, but it goes away fast. And those relationships. I'm seeing the president at other trade groups and all of a sudden you don't see those people anymore and don't exchange communications with them. That's the difficult part, I think."

Business owners should be prepared for and expect that relationships built around the business will necessarily change and even fade away when the business is no longer an anchor.

Appendices

The research project that served as the foundation for this book was focused on the emotional side of selling a business. In the course of the interviews, a number of business tips for people selling a business were discussed. A few are included here.

In addition, a top-line summary of the truths of selling a business is included. A summary of what was learned can be found near the front of the book on page 17. If someone is in a hurry or unlikely to pick up the entire book and read it, share these truths and share the summary. Spend time in the book for evidence and the receipts for these statements.

Finally, there is a list of the industries represented by the respondents interviewed. While many industries are missing, the lessons of business owners who sold seemed similar regardless of the industries served.

Miscellaneous Tips for Owners Who Want to Sell

This book's purpose is to identify and document the emotional side of selling a business. While not necessarily emotional, the business owners interviewed identified several lessons learned the hard way that could help owners through the sales process and its aftermath. Here are a few.

1. COBRA: Continuation of Health Coverage, or COBRA, is automatically offered to departing employees, including business owners who walk away. It doesn't cost the company anything since the departing employee pays the full cost of insurance out of pocket. Since most company policies are superior to, and less expensive than, health insurance on the private market, including, and especially, the Affordable Care Act programs (known as Obamacare), it's beneficial for owners to utilize COBRA for as long as possible. Many are surprised to learn that COBRA can be negotiated to apply longer than the standard expiration. These negotiations should occur before walking away from the company. After leaving, there is no longer any leverage to extend COBRA.

2. Email and File Storage: Many business owners blend their personal email and file storage accounts with their company accounts because it's easier to manage that way. However, once the owner walks away from his company, there is no guarantee that the company will allow a transition period for separating personal and business accounts. It seems that the larger the acquiring company, and the more bureaucratic the IT department, the greater the likelihood of an immediate severing of the departing owner's access. Thus, it's a good idea to set up personal email and cloud storage (e.g., Dropbox) accounts far in advance of selling the company. Begin moving personal email and files out of company accounts. This takes time, which is why it needs to begin early in the process.

3. Credit Cards: Another area where business owners often mix business and personal accounts is credit cards. Complete separation should occur before the sales process begins. In addition, some credit cards that owners might have opened as "business" cards, but shifted over time to personal use, may be closed by bank action when the owner exits the business. This can mean the loss of a card with a high credit limit. There can also be a number of autopay accounts assigned to the card that must be moved to a new card.

4. Guarantees: If the business owner made any personal guarantees along the way, such as a building note, vehicle notes, leases, etc., these should immediately be transferred to the buyer when the transaction is complete.

5. Verbal Agreements: When the business owner stays on, he might receive verbal agreements from the people he reports to regarding any number of items. Business owners have learned the hard way that these need to be confirmed in writing and documented. Some managers make casual promises that are later rescinded by the manager who claims no recollection of any promise whatsoever.

6. Personal Assets: The need to exclude personal items, such as office taxidermy, from the sale of the business is discussed in the book. Beyond items in the office, business owners should sell to themselves, liquidate, or clear the title for any assets purchased through the company, such as boats and second homes. This seems obvious, but many business owners overlook these items until due diligence and, in one case when it was missed, after the transaction closed.

7. Technology Products: Phones, laptops, and software are other items to separate. Many IT departments will want to install their software on all laptops and phones. Business owners have learned the hard way that allowing this means ceding control over their devices. Just as business owners need to secure a separate, personal cloud storage solution, they should also make certain they have access to and control over their hardware. One business owner's personal laptop was locked by the IT department after he left the company and while he was traveling overseas. For Windows machines, business owners should make sure they have a printed copy of their BitLocker drive encryption keys.

8. Relocation: Locally focused owners may find it challenging to remain in their towns, especially if it's small- to mid-sized. If the community associates the company with the owner, that association is unlikely to change post-sale. If quality, policies, or pricing changes in a way the local population resents, the owner may feel the brunt of customer anger and the frustration of being unable to do much about it. For this reason, some owners relocate after selling their local businesses.

9. Carryovers: Accrued vacation and other benefits might not be credited to the employees of a purchased business. This can be negotiated as part of the sale so that the tenure of employees, vacation days, and other benefits are carried over to the new company.

10. Severance: Business owners who plan to stay on can negotiate generous severance packages for themselves and their key employees should the buyer terminate their services for any reason other than criminal activity. This is another item that will not be offered. It must be requested and negotiated.

50 Truths About Selling a Business

1. A number of reasons might lead an owner to decide to sell. An owner may have more than one reason to make the big move.

2. No matter what the reasons for selling a business, the decision must be right for the seller, personally. Selling a business is likely the most important financial move the business owner will make. If the reasons to sell aren't right, the best decision is not to sell.

3. Many owners expressed multiple reasons for selling, but these collective reasons weren't enough to motivate them to seek a buyer. Many owners said there was one overriding reason (i.e., a catalyst) that set the sales process in motion.

4. No matter what, one day a business will either cease to exist or will continue in a capacity that is no longer under the founder's control. Business owners need to understand that nothing lasts forever.

5. For some owners, the decision to keep one's business and run it perpetually is the absolute right choice, especially when the owner derives significant non-monetary value and satisfaction from running the business.

6. Choosing to sell a business strictly because a lot of money is offered (i.e., the owner is "money whipped") isn't always the best choice, especially for younger business owners who aren't prepared to release control.

7. It's okay to plan to stay and work in the business post-sale, but business owners should be aware that employment under the new ownership may not work.

8. The longer a business owner is self-employed, the greater the chance he is unemployable.

9. Re-investments, equity rolls, and earn-outs are fine and can be lucrative. However, the business owner must be happy with the money received at close. Betting on what may come can be disappointing.

10. Owners who subtly communicate to employees that "One day this business will be for sale" had a much easier time notifying their staff that the business had been sold.

11. Employees are generally happy for the owner when they learn the business has sold, but quickly transfer their loyalty from the old owner to the new one who signs their paychecks.

12. Business owners worry about confidentiality during the process of selling their businesses. In reality, leaked information is seldom a major issue.

13. A business owner should develop a plan for addressing employees during the sales process if and when employees learn the business is for sale.

14. Employees will "guess" the business is for sale based on loose interpretations of occurrences and happenings. They will make more than ten erroneous guesses for every correct one.

15. Business owners commonly bring key employees into the process to help with due diligence.

16. Business owners who bring long-term employees and managers into the process before close typically experience less anxiety when announcing the sale of the business.

17. Due diligence is difficult regardless of whether or not an owner is prepared. And no matter how good an owner's intentions, being prepared is not always possible.

18. Owners with employees or family members involved in gathering information during due diligence appear to experience less stress and a smoother process.

19. Owners who managed both the operation of the business and due diligence reported extremely high levels of stress and anxiety during the due diligence process.

20. Signing a letter of intent is often the most exciting part of the sale because it's all promise and no pain. For many owners, it's the end of one emotional roller coaster and the start of a second one.

21. Relief was the most common response when asked how a business owner felt when the transaction closed.

22. Relief from the sale of the business comes in many flavors... relief that the process is over, relief that the responsibilities of business ownership are over, relief from the elimination of personal obligations, and relief from the risk of somehow losing everything before the business could be sold were all cited as reasons for relief.

23. Business owners who attempt the sale of their businesses without utilizing professionals tend to make mistakes and leave money on the table. At the very minimum, they should hire an attorney with M&A experience.

24. Business owners who utilized the services of a negotiator, whether a business broker, investment banker, or M&A advisor, generally felt better about the overall process of selling the business as well as the terms and conditions of the sale, including the sale price.

25. Surprisingly, many businesses sell for more than "fair market value," especially to private equity, which is often under pressure to make a number of acquisitions in a relatively short period of time

26. Many business owners felt that selling to a larger entity would lead to business innovations and capital investment.

27. Many business owners found it frustrating when the new owners had a different vision for the business post-transaction.

Sometimes the buyer failed to communicate the vision through the acquisition process. Sometimes the buyer hadn't formulated a complete vision or changed it down the road.

28. It's not easy, and often impossible, during the sales process for owners to stop and reflect on what they will do after the sale of the business. Yet, it's important to have a post-sale life plan.

29. Many business owners feel guilty about their employees when selling their businesses. Guilt shouldn't be part of the equation. Selling a business is the payoff from the hours, hard work, risk, good decisions, and leadership that went into making the business attractive to buyers.

30. It's not unusual for business owners to experience second thoughts and remorse over the sale of their businesses. In all cases, the proceeds from the sale mitigated some or all of the remorse.

31. Very few business owners wished they hadn't sold, including those with some level of remorse.

32. Owners struggled with a loss of identity after walking away from the company they once owned, especially extroverts. Some found it necessary to think through how they would introduce themselves to others post-transaction. At least one former owner wrote a script to help with this emotional hurdle.

33. Emotions regarding taxes varied. Everyone who sells a business pays taxes and pays more than he feels is "fair." Business owners who invested early in a reliable tax CPA reported less stress and anxiety about taxes.

34. Owners who prepared emotionally early on for the net proceeds, not the gross proceeds, were happier about the sale price and less enraged by taxes.

35. Many business owners are reluctant to bring buyers into their office because employees might suspect the business is for sale. Thus, many owners give buyers after-hours facility tours.

36. Buyers will perform extensive due diligence. Turnabout is fair play, and business owners shouldn't be afraid to perform due diligence on a buyer, especially if they plan to stay on and work with them.

37. Business owners who sold and remained active as a consultant or mentor to the new owner generally seemed happier than those who left immediately.

38. The actual day of close tends to be very anticlimactic.

39. Loss of control or loss of autonomy is difficult for former owners who stay with the business post-transaction.

40. The general loss of purpose is a common feeling among former owners after leaving employment post-transaction.

41. Men who maintained some level of active, not passive or investment, income post-employment were generally happier. The amount of investment income seems irrelevant. Presumably, this is related to the way males view their worth as a function of the income they generate.

42. Former owners should be prepared for long-term customers to be disappointed, especially when the former owner and customer have personal interactions and/or a personal relationship.

43. Employees and customers who felt like friends to the business owner may quickly fade from their lives, especially if they're located in different cities.

44. It is possible to remain friends with select long-term employees and customers.

45. Some business owners were disappointed when employees failed to show appreciation for their stewardship and support through the years.

46. Doubt that a business will sell is common, right up to the close. Yet, businesses do sell. It happens daily. Somewhere, every day, a business sells. Business owners should begin the process with the confidence that their business will sell.

47. Businesses do sell, but transactions also fall through. Although the business owner should proceed with confidence that his transaction will close, he should be prepared for the possibility that it will not... for now.

48. The sale of a business does not mean the end of the owner's purpose or contributions. The sale of the business is merely the end of one chapter in life and the beginning of a new one.

49. Selling a business is a series of emotional roller coasters. Business owners who could turn to a trusted friend, consultant, or mentor for guidance (beyond their professional team) were more emotionally stable.

50. All former owners wanted "the best" for their employees. While not all transactions improved their lives, in the vast majority of cases, the employees were okay.

Industries Represented Among the Respondents

Nearly 100 business owners who sold their businesses (and a few who went through parts of the process but decided not to sell) were interviewed for this book. In addition, sellers' representatives, or the people who guide others through the sale in the role of investment bankers and mergers & acquisitions advisors, were interviewed to gain their perspectives. Finally, a select number of business buyers were interviewed. The seller's representatives and buyers were few in number, but each represented dozens to hundreds of transactions.

All respondents were promised anonymity. Responses were occasionally edited to preserve confidentiality, with individual and company names changed. Both men and women were interviewed, but the pronouns used in the generic sense were masculine.

Industries represented:

- Advertising
- Architecture
- Association Management
- Automotive Repair
- Building Construction
- Business Services
- Civil Engineering
- Commercial Air Conditioning
- Consulting
- Distribution
- Drain Cleaning
- Drone Photography
- Duct Cleaning
- Engineering Design
- Farming
- Fast Food
- Food Processing
- Franchises
- Fresh Produce
- Fuel Oil Delivery
- Garage Doors

- General Contracting
- Government Contracting
- Heating, Ventilation, and Air Conditioning
- Home Security
- IT Services
- Jewelry
- Marketing
- Oil
- Packaged Goods
- Pharmacy
- Plumbing
- Publishing
- Radio
- Refrigeration
- Restaurants
- Retail
- Roofing
- Sheds
- Sign Manufacturing and Installation
- Software
- Training
- Veterinary Practices
- Video Production

About Brandon Jacob, CPA

Brandon Jacob is an independent mergers & acquisitions (M&A) consultant and CPA with over 30 years of experience on both the buy-side and sell-side. A Texas Certified Public Accountant with experience in public accounting and venture capital, Brandon has conducted valuations and/or guidance in more than 2,500 business transactions across the United States. Today, he focuses on assisting small to mid-sized service-contracting business owners prepare for and execute successful exits and generational transitions with a personalized one-on-one approach. Brandon holds a degree from Texas A&M's May School of Business. He can be contacted by email at Brandon@ContractorsCFO.com or by phone at 713.443.8311. Find Brandon on the web at www.ContractorsCFO.com.

About Matt Michel

Matt Michel is a serial entrepreneur. He founded a national franchise organization which he grew to 65 locations before exiting. Subsequently, he founded a business alliance that he grew to 5,400 member companies across the United States, Canada, and Australia before selling to private equity. Today, Matt spends time writing and speaking. With his wife, Pam, he splits time between their ranch and their lake house outside of Dallas. Matt holds an undergraduate degree from the Texas A&M College of Engineering and an MBA from the University of North Texas. Matt can be contacted by email at MattMichel@Mail.com or by phone at 214.995.8889.

www.ingramcontent.com/pod-product-compliance
Lightning Source LLC
Chambersburg PA
CBHW060505090426
42735CB00011B/2119